Cooking Well

Osteoporosis

Cooking Well

Osteoporosis

Chef Marie-Annick Courtier

Dedication

To my mother
You are my inspiration
                    —Chef Marie

COOKING WELL: OSTEOPOROSIS

Hatherleigh Press is committed to preserving and protecting the natural resources of the Earth. Environmentally responsible and sustainable practices are embraced within the company's mission statement.

Hatherleigh Press is a member of the Publishers Earth Alliance, committed to preserving and protecting the natural resources of the planet while developing a sustainable business model for the book publishing industry.

www.hatherleighpress.com

DISCLAIMER
This book offers healthy eating suggestions for educational purposes only. In no case should it be a substitute for, nor replace, a healthcare professional. Consult your healthcare professional before starting any new diet.

Library of Congress Cataloging-in-Publication Data

Courtier, Marie-Annick.
  Cooking well. Osteoporosis / Marie-Annick Courtier.
    p. cm.
  Includes bibliographical references.
  ISBN 978-1-57826-302-8 (pbk. : alk. paper) 1. Osteoporosis--Diet therapy. 2. Osteoporosis--Prevention. 3. Osteoporosis--Diet therapy--Recipes. I. Title. II. Title: Osteoporosis.
RC931.O73C693 2009
641.5'63--dc22
                          2009010620

Cooking Well: Osteoporosis is available for bulk purchase, special promotions, and premiums. For information on reselling and special purchase opportunities, call 1-800-528-2550 and ask for the Special Sales Manager.

Cover design by Nick Macagnone
Photo by Catarina Astrom
10 9 8 7 6 5 4 3 2 1

Improve your life. Change your world.

We have long known that proper nutrition plays an important role in guarding health and preventing the onset of disease. The *Cooking Well* series was created to help you learn more about the important role of nutrient-rich meals when living with your particular disorder. With *Cooking Well*, you will discover that there are many enjoyable ways to prepare delightful, great-tasting meals that are packed with a variety of healthful benefits.

Chef Marie-Annick Courtier, a well-known culinary and health expert, has utilized her background in nutrition and health studies to create easy to prepare meals that are good for you and so delicious that you and your entire family can enjoy them together. Chef Marie was born in Paris, where she acquired a knowledge of fresh, flavorful food that she incorporates into her healthy recipes. Today, Chef Marie is a widely-published author who also owns and operates a personal chef service.

Hatherleigh has a long history of providing our readers with books that help people improve their lives, whether through exercise, nutrition, or mental well-being. We are pleased to share with you the message of good health in the *Cooking Well* series.

—Andrew Flach, Publisher

Table of Contents

Part I:

Understanding Osteoporosis

Chapter 1

Living with Osteoporosis

According to the National Osteoporosis Foundation, 85 to 90 percent of adult bone mass is acquired by age 18 in girls and by age 20 in boys. It stands to reason then, that embracing a healthy diet and exercise routine in our childhood is very important in order to prevent osteoporosis later in life. An estimated 44 million Americans are at risk today. Osteoporosis can strike at any age and should not be considered only a disease for old people. The disease weakens the bones, which then can break easily. Back pain, loss of height, stooped posture and fractured bones (vertebral column, hip, rib, or wrist) are some of the most common symptoms of osteoporosis disease. Eighty percent of people with osteoporosis are women, particularly postmenopausal, and 20 percent are men over the age of 70.

Many medical reports show that **eating a healthy diet can make a huge difference in the prevention of osteoporosis or in the condition of patients with the disease.** Since maintaining strong, healthy bones is a priority, it is necessary to choose a well-balanced diet and exercise routine. The diet must offer an array of multiple nutrients, vitamins and minerals, with special emphasis on Calcium, Vitamin D, Vitamin K, Magnesium, Phosphorous, Boron, Manganese, Zinc, Copper, and Silicon. A pregnant woman should particularly pay attention to her calcium intake, in order to supply the appropriate amount, not only for her body, but also for the growing baby.

Maintaining the right level of acidity in our bodies may also play an important role in the health of our bones and in preventing the possible development of osteoporosis. Scientists are further researching this theory. Medications and the interactions between them may also have negative effects on osteoporosis and should be carefully evaluated with a physician.

People with osteoporosis often report considerable improvement in their well-being once they change their eating habits. But dieting is not the only thing, exercising plays an important role as well. Walking, swimming, biking (tri-cycle or stationary bike), light weight lifting, resistance and strengthening exercises, yoga, reflexology, balance and posture exercises, Pilates, or Tai Chi are all easy on the body and help promote healthy bones and even re-build bone density. For people with osteoporosis avoiding too much protein (high intake promotes calcium excretion in urine), too much sodium (promotes calcium excretion in urine), too much caffeine (can reduce the absorption of calcium), carbonated drinks (phosphoric acid promotes calcium loss), smoking, and alcohol abuse (which damages our cells) are imperative. One other important factor is to properly monitor the disease with your doctor. He or she should be aware of your family history, your lifestyle (including physical activity and diet), general health (blood test and hormonal levels), medications, and supplements you take in order to be able to help you with your specific needs. A bone density test should be performed every year, particularly for menopausal women and elderly men.

As with many diseases, lifestyle factors are also extremely important and we will explore these below.

Lifestyle

Many people struggling with diseases, weight problems, or allergies, often don't make the connection between their eating habits and their lifestyle choices. They often do not realize how much their emotions influence everything they do in their life, including the food they eat or finding excuses not to exercise. Unfortunately those emotions can trigger eating habits that will be the cause for more pain, worse symptoms, and be very detrimental to their health.

Consequently, **it is imperative that each individual look into his or her lifestyle and emotions to see how they affect food choices.** It is recommended that you do this with your physician, registered dietitian, psychologist, or care giver.

Osteoporosis patients should not smoke, as tobacco negatively impacts many of the body's organs and is the leading cause of lung cancer. If you do smoke and have trouble quitting, consult your physician and psychologist. Here are a few tricks to get you started on improving your health. Begin by looking into your daily routine to identify bad eating habits. Example: At work, do you drink three or four cups of coffee during the day? Do you drink too much when you entertain or go out with friends? Do you snack on mostly salted foods? Do you eat foods that you crave, knowing they are not good for you? Do you drink soda when eating lunch out? Those are just a few examples to get you thinking about what you do on a daily basis.

Chapter 2

How the Right Diet Can Help

Eating well can make a big difference in how you feel. But how should you begin to make a change, and how will you know what steps to take? Start to think about the time you felt well and when you started not to feel well. Review your journal to see what you did in the last 48 hours: what you ate, what you drank, if you ate out, if you over-exercised, did not exercise, worked too hard, and skipped or changed your medicine. If you are no longer keeping a journal, it is time to start again. You may consult your last journal, which might give you clues as to why you are not feeling well. Is it possible that an emotional event (divorce, loss of someone) or a stressful situation triggered the problem? Is a situation making you irritable or frustrated? Are you anxious about a situation, such as moving? Did you go off your diet? Did you have sleepless nights or wake up many times for different reasons? Did you fall? Has the

Avoiding Falls

Avoiding falls is essential for osteoporosis patients. Pay attention to your surroundings when walking or exercising. Sit down and get up carefully. Be particularly careful on wet areas such as during rainfall, snowfall, or when on any wet surface. Pay particular attention to your movements when taking a bath, as often sliding will result in a fall and broken bones. Watch your step when going up stairs, in or out of rides, or over a curb, and when bicycling or using exercise equipment. You should also be careful when putting on or taking off your clothes. Even a slight hit on an end table or someone hitting you by accident can result in fractures. So be aware of your surroundings.

weather changed dramatically? A number of patients have reported having more back and joint pains a few days before or after weather changes. Watch for seasonal changes and try to relax more during those times by incorporating an hour-long nap into your day. Watch your diet closely. Did you forget to drink milk or is your calcium intake not on target? Are you depressed for any reason? Do you have sexual tension? Are you constipated to the point where you are not feeling well? Sometimes the answer is right in front of you and a little thinking can provide the answers.

Once you figure it out, make sure you watch out for that situation in order to avoid repeating it. On the other hand, you might not immediately discover the reason for your crisis. You need to have patience, as it may take you a while to do so. Maintaining a positive attitude and having a strong will to determine the reason why you are not feeling well is extremely important.

A Word on Food Allergies and Sensitivities

As was mentioned earlier, determining your food allergies and sensitivities are extremely important. Consult your physician. One aspect a physician may not approach with you is the potential reasons behind those allergies or sensitivities. Our brain has many ways to tell us things or warn us. One of these is when an emotional event is attached to a particular food or scent, which can result in triggering a sudden allergy or sensitivity to that particular food or scent. The sensitivity does not necessarily surface at the time of the emotional event, but can be triggered later on in life. Our brain attaches the new event to the old event, and suddenly the allergy or sensitivity appears. Many events can be connected to the old event before something may even happen. Identifying those events in our lives can make a huge difference. Identifying the initial event in our lives that triggers the emotional chain will eventually lead to a breakthrough that may make the allergy or sensitivity disappear. The event can be related to our early childhood. Discuss this with your psychologist as he or she may be able to identify those moments, help you get over them and, consequently, eliminate certain allergies or food sensitivities. Be aware though that some allergies are truly immune system responses and are not connected to our emotions.

Revise your strategies, goals, and any notes that you made for establishing your healthier lifestyle

If you avoid certain foods due to sensitivities or allergies, it is important to remember that you may deprive your body of major nutrients. This could be the reason why you do not feel well. Consult your physician or registered dietitian to see if you need to take vitamin and mineral supplementation. Review your diet with them carefully. If you have a caregiver, talk about your findings, as he/she can help you out as well.

Talk to your family and friends. Take the time to explain your diet and how it will benefit everyone, not just you. Tell them that if you get worse, you will no longer be able to take care of chores, will be less involved with family life and with social activities you need for your own mental stability. However do not abuse such a right to avoid your own responsibilities. To recover faster, you want to keep moving a bit, so choose one chore you particularly enjoy. If you enjoy cooking, have everyone else do the prepping and cleaning, and choose quick recipes that don't require much lifting and are easy on your body. A positive attitude will make everyone much happier and enable all to live less stressful lives, which is very important for osteoporosis patients and everyone around them. Yes, it is about you and everyone around you.

Let your caregiver, helpers, or family members know you need their support for the long run. Keep in mind that the comfort and kindness of friends can go a long way and should be appreciated and treasured. Treat them with respect and even to a "special treat" once in awhile, as a small gesture can do wonders.

Do not feel intimidated to tell your friends what you can or cannot eat. They are your friends—they love you, and will understand. The last thing a real friend should do is not care for your health! **When you are feeling well, you can even write your own cook book with the foods that make you feel good and share it with your friends.** Read and educate yourself on osteoporosis. Read about the food that people with osteoporosis have reported helped them. See if it helps you as well.

Be aware that psychological and physical stress often results in fatigue, pains, and reduced abilities. One way to help you through difficult times of stress is through relaxation techniques and even mild exercises such as yoga. And don't forget about a nice refreshing bath, which can be very soothing. But be very cautious when entering and exiting the tub, to avoid falls, which often cause broken bones. Take some time off and pamper yourself!

Part II

The Importance of Nutrition

Chapter 3

Dietary Suggestions for a Healthy Lifestyle

No matter what your health problems, eating healthy foods should be a priority and a pleasant experience as well. You need to be responsible for your own health, don't expect anyone to keep you in line. As a matter of fact, many people will offer you foods that are not good for you and it is ultimately up to you to say "no, thank you." Pay particular attention to your nutrition plan and do everything in your power to stay as close to it as possible. You will feel much better, be able to enjoy your daily activities and reduce the risk of pains and, ultimately, of worsening your disease.

Eating habits are difficult to change and are often rooted in years of cultural and family habits. **Expecting a quick change is not realistic.** Patience and a strong will to change over time are a must. By employing new habits, you will eventually see the fruits of your labor in an improved overall well-being.

Healthy eating is not about eating everything you like. It is about giving your body what it needs and what agrees with it. It is about eating the right amount of calories per day considering your daily activities. Eating healthy is also about meal rituals. That means having regular meals at the same times every day. Three to four meals a day is recommended. That includes a snack in the afternoon, which is important to keep your blood sugar level stable if you have a late dinner. **It is ultimately up to you to decide what works best for your body and how to spread your meals throughout your day. Remember to appropriately divide your daily calories.** We will explore this further in the nutrition section when we specifically discuss which foods osteoporosis patients should eat and which they should avoid.

Eating Organic

Everyone knows that eating foods that are free of pesticides, chemicals, antibiotics, colorings, or hormones is better for you. This is strongly recommended for osteoporosis patients. If you are not financially strained, make an effort to shop organic at your local farmers' market, growers, and stores. If budget is an issue, do not stress about it. Sometimes we have to make practical decisions and, understandably, eating organic may not always be a priority. Also, keep in mind that due to very strict regulations, many farmers and growers are not able to obtain the organic label. But they are still producing foods that are free of pesticides, chemicals, antibiotics, and hormones, and are of excellent quality. All you need to do is find those products in your local stores and read their labels carefully.

Here are some buying tips that are economically prudent while also being healthier for you and your family. When buying dry, canned, or frozen products you should make sure to buy organic. They are not much more expensive and are much healthier for you. While you should not be eating such products on a regular basis, they can be helpful during the winter months, when a variety of vegetables and fruits are not available. Also if you cook for yourself and feel physically exhausted, you might opt for the dry, canned or frozen product.

Reduce your individual portions, particularly with meat products. You can stretch your dollars while you shrink your waistline. Portion sizes at your local store are often larger than what you really need to eat. For example, a chicken breast often weighs 8 ounces when you should only be eating about 4 ounces.

Support your local farmers and growers. The more distance the food travels from farm to table, the greater the cost.

Join a food co-op. Co-ops purchase food in bulk and often carry organic items. If there isn't one in your town, consider starting one with family and friends.

Share your knowledge. If you have discovered healthy organic or non-organic foods from a reputable supplier, pass the news on via an e-mail to osteoporosis organizations and friends. They will appreciate it immensely and you will help promote such suppliers, which eventually will be in a better position to lower prices based on demand.

Eating Out

Preferably, you should eat out no more than twice a week. Keep that time for the weekend with family and friends. Too many places use commercially packaged food and unhealthy fats, which are detrimental to your health. Not to mention how much salt is in those foods—and you might not get enough calcium either! It is extremely important that you pay attention to the type of foods you choose when going out.

In a restaurant, do not hesitate to question the waiter about the ingredients in a particular dish. Let him/her know you are on a specific diet and looking for high calcium dishes that are also low-fat. More and more chefs are willing to accommodate their clients today because they know it is important for the survival of the restaurant. There is also an increased demand for healthier choices, and the industry is paying attention. Choosing a restaurant that caters to foods closer to your diet is also wise—chances are you will find more food that you can enjoy there in the first place (e.g. Italian, Mediterranean, or vegetarian restaurants).

Quick Tips for Ordering at a Restaurant

- Order steamed vegetables with olive oil or lemon on the side
- Brown rice is also safe
- Ask for your dish to be prepared with a little olive oil, canola oil, or grapeseed oil, and no butter. Ask for olive oil and vinegar on the side for your salad dressing or bring your own dressing. Half a lemon is also a good substitute for dressing or butter on steamed vegetables.
- Half a baked potato is safe as long as it is without toppings and butter (you can always drizzle a little olive oil over it yourself).
- Stay away from unhealthy carbohydrates and ask to substitute steamed vegetables instead. Avoid most desserts except fresh fruits. It is best to save your sweet tooth for homemade, healthier goodies.
- Don't blindly eat what is served to you—pay attention to the type of food and the amount of food, and try to figure out the total calories. Put that into perspective with your meal allowance.

When visiting with family or friends, make them aware of your health situation a few days before the visit. If they already know, just give them a quick phone call to remind them, as many people have a very active lifestyle and may easily forget. Be very diligent and carefully choose what you eat. If needed, ask the host if he or she made the food from scratch, what is in it, or if it is store bought food. And remember: when in doubt, do not eat it. If you are not sure of the situation, you can always eat before you go to an event. If you know that the food the host will prepare will not agree with you, you can ask if you can bring your own food. No one should get upset; after all it is about making sure everyone enjoys the party!

While traveling, keep the same attitude that you have when you are eating out close to home. Be even more vigilant. It is best to bring your own food, but sometimes this is not possible (such as when traveling by airplane.)When booking your flight, most airlines will gladly reserve a low-fat meal for you. Vegetarian meals may be good, as they are often based on cheese and carbohydrates. Ask specifically what foods are included in the meals. At the airport, look for food that is freshly prepared in front of you and as close as possible to your nutritional plan. Take with you enough snack foods to last you a day or two in case of schedule delays. Nuts, raisins, and dates are easy to carry. You will be able to find bottles of water or milk in most places.

When traveling abroad, be even more careful than you would be at home. Foods are not prepared the same way and many unknown ingredients may be a real problem to your health. Stick with plain grilled, steamed, broiled, or baked main courses with rice, potatoes, or steamed vegetables as side dishes. If you have no choice, pick the healthiest option and eat what you know is safe for you. Be careful with raw foods, as sanitation may not be as thorough as at home. Always ask for a bottle of water to be opened in front of you. Don't miss the opportunity to go to a local market and purchase some fresh fruits, vegetables, and healthy snacks such as almonds, walnuts, hazelnuts, dates, or whatever you may be able to keep in your hotel room.

Don't forget to wash the vegetables and fruits with a bottle of water mixed with a little vinegar. This will help kill bacteria not visible to the eye. If you have a refrigerator in the room, stock it with milk, yogurt, or cheese to meet your daily calcium needs. Read all food labels carefully. If you don't understand the language, this may be a problem. See if the concierge or a person speaking your language at the hotel can assist you. Be on your guard at all times. If you take supplements or specific medications, make sure you have enough for your trip, plus a week's worth as back-up. Standards overseas are not always the same as in the United States.

Chapter 4

Foods to Avoid, Foods to Choose

Nutrition

To improve your health, you need to take care of yourself and the first step is to respect your body by giving it the food that will benefit it the most. Your meals should include a wide selection of fresh wholesome foods to satisfy not only your personal taste, but also your nutritional needs. Eating a variety of food is also important to avoid boredom and get the proper nutrients. As explained earlier, it is not always easy particularly during the winter when certain vegetables and fruits are not available or when you don't feel well. Substitution with organic frozen or canned foods is then necessary and only encouraged during such times.

You may also have to take into consideration your food sensitivities or allergies. At first, this can be difficult to deal with. Take time to think and be patient, soon you will realize it is not really a big deal and there are many ways to deal with it. If you think you may have allergies and have not yet been tested, be sure to contact your medical provider. This is very important as often foods can trigger aching pains, weakness, headaches, and many other symptoms.

When dealing with food sensitivities or allergies, think about how you can replace the offending food with something that you like and that has similar, if not healthier, nutritional values. For example, you can't eat cow milk, which is an important source of calcium that osteoporosis patients need, and you love cream of broccoli. Just substitute fortified unsweetened soy milk for cow milk in your favorite recipe—problem solved! Be aware, though, that soy milk does not offer the same nutrition value as cow milk. Look for a brand that has Vitamin A, Vitamin D, and Calcium added.

How much food should you eat? For sure, most of us have a natural desire to eat more than we really need. Knowing that, all we have to do is be sure to eat less and watch out for the food that our body does not really need or should not receive. It may be a simple formula, but it is very effective.

So which foods would be most beneficial to an osteoporosis patient? As was said earlier, the secret lies in choosing a vast diversity of foods, the right amount of food, and the foods that agree with you. Eating more foods that contain anti-inflammatory properties will also be beneficial. To select the right foods for your body, you need to understand the basics of nutrients. Here is some very basic information to help you out.

Carbohydrates area main source of energy for the body (calories) and are necessary for the proper use of fats by the body. Complex carbohydrates are better for you and are found in many grains, dried beans, sweet potatoes, potatoes, corn, or cream of millet. Fibrous complex carbohydrates are found in broccoli, carrots, cauliflower, green beans, peppers, spinach, zucchini, and many other vegetables. Simple carbohydrates are found in many sugary items such as cereals, breakfast bars, crackers, candies, and many commercial desserts. Those are not healthy for you. On the other hand, simple carbohydrates found in small amounts in fruits such as apples, bananas grapefruit, oranges, pears, pineapples, or peaches are healthy for you and should be part of your daily allowances. Unrefined carbohydrates can possibly be a problem for some osteoporosis patients and are found in brown rice, wheat flour, and many products containing wheat. These can be important in a diet as they help eliminate waste and substitution needs to be explored carefully.

Fats are an indispensable part of every cell. They are a source of energy (calories), supply essential fatty acids and carry fat-soluble vitamins. Hormones are manufactured from fats, which make healthy fats indispensable to the good functioning of our body and even promote weight loss. Fats are also a good source of lubrication for the joints. There are three types of fats: saturated, polyunsaturated, and monounsaturated.

- *Saturated fats* are fats that raise bad cholesterol levels and are associated with heart disease. They are solid at room temperature and are found in animal products such as meat, poultry, eggs, dairy, packaged foods, and solid shortenings. The worst of these is hydrogenated fat (or partially hydrogenated), also called trans fat, which is found in many processed foods and should be eliminated from your diet. Check labels carefully. Coconut oil, palm oil, and non-dairy creamers contain high levels of saturated fats and should be eliminated as well.

- *Unsaturated fats (monounsaturated and polyunsaturated)* are healthier for you, but keep in mind that they are still fats, and that you should carefully control your daily intake. Monounsaturated fats have one double bond in their chemical structure and are liquid at room temperature. They lower bad cholesterol and raise levels of good cholesterol. They are found in olive oil, canola oil, or avocado oil.
- *Polyunsaturated fats* have two or more double bonds in their chemical structure and are liquid at room temperature. They have positive effects on blood sugar levels, reduce inflammation, and even influence the amount of fat stored by the body. They are found in fish oil, flaxseed oil, grapeseed oil, and walnut oil.

Proteins are a good source of energy and the major building materials for all body tissues. They also help produce enzymes and hormones, which regulate the body's functions. You'll find proteins in meats, poultry, fish, eggs, dairies, dried beans, legumes, soy (edamame), tofu, and nuts. Vegetable protein and lean animal protein (chicken, turkey, fish, egg whites, and low-fat dairies) are recommended. Eating proteins containing a large amount of healthy unsaturated fat, particularly Omega-3 fatty acids, is also essential for your well-being. Those can be found in fatty fish such as salmon, tuna, sardines, or anchovies.

Vitamins are chemical compounds found in many foods which help regulate the body's functions and fight infectious diseases. Contrary to belief, vitamins do not provide energy. Vitamins B (meats, poultry, nuts, legumes, green vegetables, dairies, and whole grains) and C (citrus, berries, green vegetables, papayas, tomatoes, livers, and potatoes) are not stored in the body and need to be eaten every day. However Vitamins A (dairies, green leafy vegetables, yellow vegetables, livers, and fruits), Vitamin D (dairy products, eggs, tuna, cod, mackerel, sea bass, liver oils, and sunlight), E (vegetable oils, dark green leafy vegetables, nuts, wheat germ, and whole grains) and K (dark green leafy vegetables, alfalfa, and tomatoes) are stored by the body.

Minerals are essential for the body to function properly and play an important role in our metabolic process. Minerals do not provide energy. Calcium (milk products, salmon, broccoli, and oysters), Chromium (onion, broccoli, meat, lettuce, and grape juice), Copper (vegetables, liver, legumes, cereals, and oil), Iodine (seafood, yeast breads, dairy products, eggs, and wheat germ), Iron (beef, poultry, beans, lentils, tofu, eggs, dark green leafy vegetables, broccoli, asparagus, grains, and dried fruits), Magnesium (dark green leafy vegetables, watercress, Brazil nuts, sunflower seeds, sesame seeds, pumpkin seeds, bananas, cashews, tofu, vegetables, and legumes), Manganese (grains, cereals, tea, pineapple, strawberries, and starches), Sodium (salt), Potassium (fruits, vegetables, meat, and milk), Selenium (meat, seafood, grains, molasses, and Brazil nuts), and Zinc (oyster, meat, dairy products, eggs, and wheat germ) are all minerals.

Fibers cannot be used by the body and therefore do not supply energy. However, they are important for the proper function of the intestines and may prevent cancers. Soluble fibers slow down the absorption of food in the stomach, and may be associated with reducing blood cholesterol, and maintaining the proper blood sugar level. Soluble fibers are found in oats, dried beans, lentils, peas, fruits, and vegetables. Insoluble fibers speed the digestive system and may reduce the risk of cancers. You find them in whole grains, dried beans, cereals, brown rice, and wheat pasta.

Water is indispensable for the body to function well. Water regulates the body temperature, assists in the digestive process, and transports nutrients and waste. Water is present in mostly everything, but certain foods contain much higher amounts of water than others (watermelon is mostly water). Drink plenty of water throughout the day. Water can also be used for making tea. The best known anti-inflammatory sources for tea are white and green tea. They also help stimulate the immune system and help to get rid of free radicals which are harmful to the body. Pure organic cranberry juice, no sugar added, is helpful with urinary tract infection, but should be drunk only when necessary, as it has a negative effect on bone density. Pure organic prune juice will also help with constipation.

Every nutrient's role is to supply energy to the body. That energy is measured in calories. Carbohydrates, proteins, and fats can be used by the body to supply energy.

- 1 gram of carbohydrate supplies 4 calories
- 1 gram of protein supplies 4 calories
- 1 gram of fat supplies 9 calories

As you can see, fats contribute a lot more calories which is why you need to keep your fat intake in line to stay healthy.

Now that you understand the role of nutrients, how many do you really need to function well? **For most people, the general healthy guideline is about 1400-1500 daily calories for women and 2000 to 2100 daily calories for men.** Keep in mind that those numbers may vary based on your lifestyle, level of activity and exercise, and if you are trying to gain or lose weight. Consult your physician or registered dietitian for your adequate daily calories.

To emphasize good healthy habits, we also need a healthy meal plan. Such a plan must emphasize a low-fat diet that contains healthy fats and high fiber intake. As a guideline, a meal should contain one portion of protein-rich foods (3 to 4 ounces for women and 6 to 7 ounces for men), one or more portions of vegetables low in starch (1 cup for women and 2 cups for men), and one portion of healthy whole grains or vegetables high in starch (1/2 cup for women and 3/4 cup for men of cooked whole grains or a small potato for women and a little larger for men). If weight loss is desired, limit your carbohydrates and starches (potatoes, rice, pasta, baked beans, yams, or sweet potatoes). This includes vegetables and fruits that contain high sugar levels (corn, peas, squash, plantains, or bananas). You should also eat two portions of fruits daily, preferably with breakfast, lunch, or a snack. On a daily basis, every meal should include an organic low-fat dairy product such as low-fat milk (cow or fortified soy milk), low-fat plain yogurt, and low-fat cheeses. Finally, drink plenty of water throughout the day to hydrate and to help cleanse the body of toxins.

Osteoporosis patients must be sure to get adequate amounts of particular nutrients on a daily basis. It is best to get them from natural food sources rather than from supplements. Ask your doctor if you need to take any supplements before doing so, as it may have negative effects on your health or can interact with other medications you are taking. Here are the most important nutrients for an osteoporosis patient:

Calcium	Organic low-fat dairies, powdered milk, fortified soy products, legumes, fish eaten with bones (salmon or sardines), oysters, broccoli, asparagus, watercress, and nuts.
	If calcium supplementation is recommended by your doctor, choose a chewable or liquid supplement first as they are easily absorbed by the body. Citrate calcium is another good source. Calcium is best absorbed by the body when taken throughout the day, with a meal, and in approximately 500 to 600 mg doses at a time. You may develop gas or constipation from taking supplementation, so increase your intake of water and fibers. Flaxseeds or prunes can be helpful and you will find a prune recipe in the dessert section of this book. Make sure you talk with your doctor about the possible interaction of medicines or over the counter medicines with calcium supplementation.
Vitamin D	Sardines, salmon, tuna, herrings, mackerel, mushrooms, egg yolks, cod liver oil. Combine with calcium-rich food for best absorption. 15 minutes of sun exposure per day is also a good source of this vitamin. You may also look for products that have Vitamin D added, such as in milk, orange juice, soy milk, or cereals.

Magnesium	Dark green leafy vegetables, watercress, broccoli, avocados, Brazil nuts, sunflower seeds, sesame seeds, bananas, cashews, apples, apricots, cantaloupes, peaches, salmon, and tofu.
Phosphorous	Salmon, halibut, skim milk, low-fat dairies, chicken breast, oatmeal, broccoli, asparagus, corn, eggs, dried fruits, sesame seeds, and pumpkin seeds.
Boron	Almonds, hazelnuts, walnuts, Brazil nuts, apricots, avocados, red wine (Shiraz and Cabernet).
Manganese	Wheat germ, whole grains, nuts, shellfish, tea, low-fat dairies, apples, apricots, avocados, bananas, cantaloupe, peaches, green leafy vegetables, salmon, and tofu.
Zinc	Cooked oysters, eggs, whole grains, nuts, low-fat yogurt, fish, legumes, mushrooms, pumpkin and sunflower seeds, sardines, and poultry.
Copper	Shellfish, nuts, seeds, whole grains, mushrooms, avocados, barley, broccoli, lentils, oats, oranges, radishes, raisins, salmon, and green leafy vegetables.
Vitamin K	Green leafy vegetables, kale, cauliflower and broccoli.
Silicon	Cereals, apples, oranges, cherries, raisins, almonds, raw cabbage, onions, carrots, pumpkin, cucumber, fish, honey, oats, unrefined grains/cereals with high fiber content, nuts and seeds.

Special Comments

Red meats are not prohibited but should be eaten occasionally. You may treat yourself every two weeks with 3 ounces of organic beef (for women) and 4 ounces of organic beef (for men). It is best to substitute beef with buffalo, venison, ostrich, or elk, which have less saturated fat. Buffalo and venison are very similar in taste to beef. Lamb, liver, kidney, heart, or tongue may also be eaten on rare occasion. Make sure the meat is always from an organic source.

Shellfish such as shrimp, crabs, lobsters, oysters, snails, mussels, clams, and scallops are not prohibited for those who have no cholesterol problems. They can be easily enjoyed once a week in soups, salads, or entrees.

Preferably organic canned or frozen foods are permissible when some seasonal products are not available or when you are not up to preparing fresh food. Organic is preferable. If purchasing non-organic, watch for hydrogenated fats or unhealthy fats, flours, sodium, thickeners, colorings, preservatives, additives,

Foods to Avoid

Osteoporosis patients should particularly avoid the following substances and foods due to their negative effect on calcium retention in the body:

- High amount of protein
- Sodium
- Caffeine
- Soda and carbonated drinks
- Smoking
- Foods high in oxalate and phytate: cacao, bitter chocolate, spinach, sorrel, celery rave, beet, rhubarb, fig, currant, 100% wheat bran, buckwheat, poppy seeds, amaranth, chard, and certain types of legumes such as pinto beans, navy beans, or peas. (As beans are a good source of plant protein, white beans may be consumed occasionally. Soak them overnight and discard the water before starting to cook. Starting with fresh water will reduce the phytate level in the cooked beans.)

For more details on which foods to eat and which to avoid, please refer to the shopping list chapter.

and any other ingredients that may cause you problems. Choose foods that are low in fat and prepared with olive oil or canola oil rather than other types of oils or butter.

Eliminate convenience foods, commercially prepared mixes, prepared packaged meals (including frozen ones) most foods from vending machines, baked goods containing refined white flour and unhealthy fats, most food bars, powders drinks, and commercial meal shakes. If you are not feeling well and cannot cook for yourself, see that your caregiver or helper does not feed you such foods, but rather prepares meals that are suitable for your needs and based on this book's recommendations. If neither of these possibilities are available to you, order fresh "home-style" meals from a couple of reliable sources. Establish a rapport with local places that offer healthy foods and that you can rely on with just a phone call. Your health is worth the time invested and, who knows, you may have fun doing it!

A word on eggs: Egg yolks contain cholesterol. If you have no problem with cholesterol, you may enjoy a whole egg. On the other hand, if you have to watch your cholesterol, use egg whites only. One whole egg equals two egg whites. Do not use commercial egg products as they may contain thickeners and can often cause allergic or sensitivity reactions.

A word on cooking chicken and turkey: Those white meats may be cooked once in awhile with the skin to preserve moisture, but do not eat the skin because it is high in fat.

A word on alcohol: Because this is a low-fat diet, digestion is much faster which causes alcohol to be absorbed faster through the bloodstream. Consequently, alcohol goes faster to the brain and people have reported lightheadedness, headache, hot sensations, a loss of mental capacities, stomach and body cramps, fatigue, confusion, or even feeling drunk and hung over after just a small amount of alcohol. Many mixed drinks and commercial mixes contain ingredients that can cause health problems. So it is best to totally stay away from alcohol.

A healthy tip on constipation: You can take 1 teaspoon to 2 teaspoons maximum of cod fish oil or flaxseed oil daily. Or you can also have up to 1 tablespoon freshly ground flaxseeds daily mixed in your food. A few prunes, pre-soaked in water for 24 hours, after a meal will also be helpful. When traveling, use pills for convenience but do so for short-term periods only. Individual flaxseed sachets might be available at your local health food stores.

Hydration and fiber also play an important role in preventing constipation. Drink lots of water throughout the day and add fiber to your meals (vegetables and fruits). Natural organic prune juice, no sugar added, is also very helpful with constipation.

Chapter 5

Tips on Shopping

Selecting Food

As we just explained, nutrition is very important and so is the food we choose. You need to be concerned with colors, shapes, flavors, textures, personal likes and dislikes, allergies and sensitivities, diet, and foods that complement each other. These factors are all important in helping to avoid sickness, boredom, and unpleasant experiences.

Colors and shapes give a dish an attractive appearance and are pleasing to the eyes. Flavors and textures excite our taste buds, which send signals to our brain and, in turn, send us back sensations. Those sensations can be good or bad. They can come to you within seconds, minutes, hours, or even over-night. During that time allergies, food sensitivities, or food poisoning can occur. Flavors need to be in harmony, not over powering, not too light. For example, acidic and tart foods as accompaniments to fatty foods help balance the taste and promote easier digestion.

Softness and firmness is what is referred to as **texture.** Vegetables taste much better when crunchy rather than mushy, and don't forget they retain more vitamins and minerals when they are not overcooked. Creating a meal with similar textures is boring and not recommended (eg. leek and potato soup, mashed potato, and meatloaf).

Personal preference is another important point because none of us will eat something we don't like. How your body responds to what you eat is equally important. No one wants to eat something that makes you sick. Likes and dislikes are important to consider when selecting foods as long as you don't forget that nutrients are even more important to your well-being. You might have to tolerate foods you dislike once in awhile for your health's sake. Find ways with herbs, spices, or sauces to camouflage the flavors of healthy foods that you don't particularly like. In other words, trick your taste buds! Here is a quick trick to deal with strong flavors that may bother you. Take, for example, cauliflower. Once cooked, cauliflower can have strong flavors that turn people off. To avoid such a problem, all you need to do is to cook the cauliflower in milk. The strong flavors will be absorbed by the milk and the cauliflower will taste milder and even sweeter. If smell is still a problem, mix the cauliflower with another ingredient such as mashed potatoes with garlic and herbs. The cauliflower flavor will disappear, but not the nutrients! If you think that way about food, you will enjoy your food much more and will have fun creating your own recipe while still enjoying all the benefits of such healthy foods. Be careful to choose combinations that make sense. In this case, it would not be advisable to experiment mixing cauliflower with mint—they don't complement each other, and taste quite awful together! As you can see, all these factors are important in selecting the right food.

Reading Labels

Strive to purchase fresh ingredients and prepare the food yourself. But from time to time, you may have to purchase organic prepared, canned, or frozen foods. If so, you must read the entire label carefully. Most packaged foods will offer important nutritional information. A label will offer nutrition facts which will be broken down into serving size, number of servings, amount per serving, calories, total fat, cholesterol, trans-fat, carbohydrates, protein, sodium, sugar, and vitamins. Be particularly aware of the fats, sodium, carbohydrates, and calcium. Vitamin D is often not shown.

For carbohydrates, you will often see two categories: fiber and sugar. Remember that sugar can come from many sources. The label should specify the origin (such as sugar, brown sugar, turbinado sugar, honey, maple sugar or syrup, sucrose, glucose, corn syrup, dextrin, confectioner's sugar, high fructose, lactose, dextrose, maltodextrin, molasses, caramel, date sugar, rice syrup, etc.) Sugar can also come from sugar alcohol: sorbitol, xylitol, lactitol, isomalt, maltitol, or mannitol. These sugars have fewer total calories than regular sugar. You will find them often in low-calorie, low-carb, reduced-carb, and even carb-free products. However, they have been found to cause various negative reactions such as nausea, headaches, diarrhea, bloating, and even allergies. You should try to stay away from those products whenever possible. Avoid aspartame and any products containing aspartame as it may cause cancer.

Be aware that manufacturers do not always report the exact numbers because they are allowed to round numbers down. If the number is less than 0.5 g, they don't have to report it either. So carefully read the list of ingredients to look for unhealthy fats, bad sugars, and other ingredients that may cause health problems.

Familiarize yourself as much as possible with labels and read carefully every time you buy a product. When shopping, take with you the list of foods and ingredients you cannot eat. When in doubt about an ingredient, do not purchase the product. Always compare nutritional ingredients among products until you are familiar with them. Once you find a brand that agrees with you, don't ever assume it will be around forever. Manufacturers are known to change a few ingredients now and then for various reasons. For example, they may find an ingredient from a cheaper source overseas. So read the label every time you purchase a product.

Here is a label example (walnut pieces):

Nutrition Facts

Serving Size 1 oz (30g)
Serving Per Container 15 Servings

Amount Per Serving	
Calories 210	Calories from fat 180

	% Daily Value*
Total Fat 20g	31%
Saturated Fat 1.5g	8%
Trans Fat 0g	
Cholesterol 0mg	0%
Sodium 0mg	
Total Carbohydrates 3g	
Dietary Fiber 3g	14%
Sugar 0g	
Protein 5g	

Vitamin A 0%	Vitamin C 0%
Calcium 2%	Iron 6%

There are 9 calories/gram of fat. Since there are 20g of fat in this product, 180 of the total calories (9X20=180) are from fat.

5% Daily Value or less is low – 20% Daily Value or more is high

Actual grams of fat in this product

It is mandatory that trans fat be listed on labels since 2006

Actual amount of cholesterol in this product

Actual amount of sodium in this product

Total of carbohydrates from various sources

Dietary fiber from the total amount of carbohydrates

Total sugar in the amount of carbohydrates listed

Total protein in this product

Shopping List

Below are three lists that can be used for osteoporosis patients' diet guidelines. You will find **"Encouraged Foods," "Questionable Foods, no more than once a week,"** and **"Prohibited Foods."** Keep in mind that everyone's metabolism is different and no one list fits all. Where one person may find relief in not eating a particular food, another person may not. Consequently, it is very important to start to work on your own personal list. The lists below are a good start to help you design your own healthy diet. A personal diet needs to be carefully designed for each individual and possibly include "vitamin and mineral" supplementation to compensate for loss of natural sources (please consult your physician). Keeping a journal is highly recommended, as it may help you determine reasons for when you are not feeling well or when you are feeling great.

Once you have established your own list of foods to avoid, you will be able to make substitutions for your recipes and enjoy your meals without any worries. Finding a balanced diet and lifestyle that makes you feel great will also make a difference in your overall sense of well-being, and you must maintain your new diet and lifestyle for the rest of your life. If you do so, your overall well-being will be enhanced permanently and, consequently, you will be able to live a more pleasurable life. Patience, perseverance, discipline, self-esteem, self-confidence, faith, engaging in relaxation techniques, and eating right are all habits that will contribute to your well-being.

	Safe and Encouraged Foods	Questionable Foods, Permissible	Prohibited Foods
Cereals/Flour/ starch	Whole grains, oats, millet, quinoa, nut flours (almond, walnut, and hazelnut), wild rice, wheat germ, whey, brown rice, barley, whole wheat pasta, chestnuts, potato, sweet potato, tapioca, whole wheat couscous, corn		Buckwheat, Amaranth, chips, crackers, many cereals, commercial products made with refined flour, refined grains, white rice and regular pasta 100% wheat bran
Fats	Olive oil, canola oil, grapeseed oil, avocado oil, flaxseed oil, walnut oil, and fish oil (high in Vitamin D)		Butter, margarine, cottonseed oil, shortening, lard, coconut oil, palm oil, and any hydrogenated oils or oiled base. Full fat dairies Bacon fat

	Safe and Encouraged Foods	Questionable Foods, Permissible	Prohibited Foods
Meat, Fish, and Eggs	White meat from turkey and chicken. Cornish hen, pheasant, and rabbit. Fish: wild salmon, tuna, sardines, herring, cod, mackerel, halibut, snapper, founder, sole, shark, mahi mahi, perch. Can salmon or tuna in water. Can sardines in olive oil or tomato sauce. Oyster. Soy and Organic eggs.	Buffalo, venison, elk, ostrich, goose, lamb, and duck. Seafood, particularly crabs, but watch for cholesterol. Organic beef	Anchovy, trout, monkfish, swordfish, surimi, commercial breaded fish and fish sticks. Dark meat (chicken and turkey), sausages, pâtés, bacon, liver, kidney, heart, and tongue. No commercial lunch meat. No eggs substitutes
Vegetables, Legumes, and Fruits	Asparagus, carrots, squash, zucchinis, broccolis, cabbage, bok choy, Chinese cabbage, potatoes, mushrooms, sweet potatoes, onions, parsley, garlic, leeks, turnips, chestnuts, peas, yams, cabbages, pumpkins, green leafy vegetables, dandelion, kale, bell peppers, fennel, peas, cauliflower, tomatoes, avocadoes, ginger, apples, pears, peaches, grapes, cherries, pineapple, mangos, cantaloupes, papayas, apricots, peaches, citrus, grapes, berries, kiwis, raisins, dates, soy, and organic natural dry fruits except those prohibited.	Dry beans (preferably white beans), lentils, and garbanzos. No more than once a week.	Fried or commercially breaded or coated with a batter vegetables, vegetables cooked in butter, vegetables bouillons or cubes, prepared vegetables containing thickeners, high fat, and high sodium. Spinach, sorrel, Swiss chard, celery rave, beet, rhubarb, fig, currant, gooseberry
Dairies	Low-fat dairies (low-fat and skim milk, buttermilk, low-fat sour cream, plain low-fat yogurt, low-fat cottage cheese, low-fat cheese, fortified rice milk, fortified soy milk, fortified almond milk	Homemade low-fat custard or pudding. Low-fat ice cream or frozen yogurt	Full fat dairies and desserts (milk, cream, butter, margarine, sour cream, whipped cream, cheese, yogurt, ice cream, cottage cheese, imitation dairies, custards, puddings, and products containing unhealthy fats.

	Safe and Encouraged Foods	Questionable Foods, Permissible	Prohibited Foods
Condiments	Particularly apple cider vinegar. Vinegars, sage and various herbs, spices, potassium salt, peppers, mustards, ketchup, hot sauce, homemade low-fat dressing		Broth cubes or dry mixes, most commercial prepared sauces and dressings, most barbecue sauces, some spices mix as they contain other unhealthy ingredients.
Desserts, Sweets, And Nuts	Maple syrup, honey, agave nectar, fruit fructose, preserves (no corn syrup) Raw almonds, walnuts, hazelnuts, pistachios, Brazil nuts, cashews, pumpkin seeds, pepitas, sesame seeds, sunflower seeds, and flaxseeds Liquorices	Fructose, dextrose, brown sugar, agar agar, marmalades, jams, homemade low-fat desserts, low-fat rice or tapioca puddings Peanut, sesame seeds	Corn syrup, Stevia, NutraSweet, Splenda, Saccharine, and any artificial sweeteners. Gelatin, all packaged commercial mixes or desserts, commercial baked goods, chewing gums, high fat desserts, sweetened and coated dried fruits, poppy seeds
Beverages and Extracts	Water, mild white tea, green tea, black tea, or herbal teas. Organic cider, homemade fruit juices, homemade concentrated fruit juices, organic prunes juice (no sugar added) 1 to 2 cups/day max. mild coffee, preferably decaffeinated	A glass of wine toward the middle or end of a meal, not on empty stomach	Sodas, high caffeine drinks, most carbonated drinks, flavored water; powdered base mixes for drinks or shakes, artificial flavored or colored drinks, coffee substitute, artificial syrups, sweetened fruit juices. Alcoholic beverages Bitter chocolate and cacao.

Chapter 6

Prepping Your Kitchen

Cooking with the Right Tools

Because you may find yourself tired, it is important for you to limit energy expenditure in the kitchen. There is no better way to do this than having the right tools to help you out. Having a food processor, electric mixer, blender, microwave, good quality knives, electric can opener, and utensils within easy reach while prepping and cooking will contribute to making your life easier. Other important tools in your kitchen are your pots and pans. A good quality pan distributes heat evenly over the entire surface and allows proper cooking. Though a heavy-gauge pan is better for cooking, it may be a problem to lift for osteoporosis patients. When looking for lighter pans, it is important that the weight of the metal be on the bottom of the pan. This allows for better conductivity and consequently better, faster cooking. Different kinds of metals are available and you should be concerned with the conductivity of heat rather than appearance.

- **Copper** is the best heat conductor, but rather expensive. Copper reacts chemically with some foods, which can have poisonous results. Lining it with another metal, such as stainless steel, avoids such problems.
- **Aluminum** is a very good conductor and commonly used. Do not use aluminum cookware for storing strong acidic foods, since it will chemically react with the food, creating poisonous compounds.
- **Calphalon**, which is made of anodized aluminum, is a better choice if you are concerned about any chemical reactions.
- **Stainless steel** is a poor heat conductor and, therefore, not recommended.

- **Cast iron** is a great conductor but can be very heavy. It holds heat for a long time, but has the disadvantage of cracking easily when hit or dropped. When you scratch and wash your pan, then dry it, you will notice a black stain on your cloth. This means that a small amount of iron can leak into your food presenting a health concern. Avoid using such pans.
- **Non-stick** such as Teflon is ideal for low-fat cooking. Make sure the surface is always perfect. One little dent will allow the metal under the Teflon layer to come into contact with the food. This can be a serious health issue. Inspect regularly and replace immediately any pans that have even the smallest scratch.
- **Earthenware** and glass are easily breakable. They are not good conductors, but resist corrosion and do not have chemical reactions with acidic foods like some metal pans do. These are good for baking casseroles, though.

Seasoning, Herbs, and Spices

You may wonder what the difference is between seasonings and flavoring, and why this is important. It is important, particularly with low-fat cooking. Since fat provides flavor and you are going to limit fat in your cooking, you need to find other ways to compensate for it and enhance your cuisine. There is no better way than by using seasonings, herbs, and spices.

Seasoning means enhancing and balancing the natural flavors of a dish by adding salt and pepper. You will notice that the recipes in this book use a very little amount of salt. The reason is that our foods are too salty these days, and you actually need very little to balance flavors and for your health. Various types of salt are available: table salt, granulated salt, coarse salt, sea salt, and mineral salt. I prefer sea salt because it is un-processed and contains important minerals and trace elements. It also gives a much better flavor to food in very small quantities. Peppers are available in many different forms: black, white, green, red, etc. It is best to freshly grind pepper to obtain a dish's full flavor.

Flavoring means adding one or more flavors to a dish without overpowering the original flavor (unless purposely done). Flavoring refers to anything other than salt and pepper, for example: lemon juice, herbs, spices, vegetables, mustard, lemon or orange peel, red or cayenne pepper (no, they do not belong to the pepper family but rather the paprika and sweet bell pepper family), low-sodium soy sauce, etc.

Herbs are the leaves of plants and spices are the buds, fruits, flowers, seeds, roots of plants and trees. Keep dried herbs and spices in a cool place, away from lights and heat (not next to the stovetop or oven) or they will spoil quickly. Keep them tightly covered. Most of the dry herbs have a shelf life of four to six months. Do not buy large quantities since you probably will not use them.

Also, buy high quality herbs—if you buy poor quality, you end up putting more in your food, and thus spending more money.

Fresh herbs with short stems should be stored in an unsealed plastic bag or wrapped in a moist paper towel. Always refrigerate herbs so they can keep up to a week. Fresh herbs with long stems should be placed in the refrigerator

Below is a list of herbs and spices that go best with certain foods.

Use a few per dish, not all. Explore them, use them, and then be adventurous and create your own combination. This is what will make you familiar with them and make your cooking experience most exciting.

Chicken
Chervil, coriander, cumin, marjoram, parsley, peppers, rosemary, sage, savory, shallot, basil, tarragon, thyme, and ginger

Beef, Buffalo, or Venison
Dill, leek, marjoram, oregano, parsley, peppers, rosemary, savory, basil, tarragon, thyme, ginger, garlic, and shallot

Veal
Leek, marjoram, oregano, parsley, peppers, rosemary, savory, basil, tarragon, thyme, ginger, garlic, and shallot

Rabbit
Oregano, parsley, peppers, rosemary, thyme, ginger, garlic, and shallot

Seafood
Anise, dill, marjoram, oregano, parsley, peppers, rosemary, sage, basil, tarragon, thyme, ginger, garlic, and shallot

Fruit
Ambrosia, anise, mint, parsley, rosemary, sage, sesame, and ginger

Vegetables
Chives, cumin, dill, leek, marjoram, mint, oregano, parsley, peppers, paprika, rosemary, sage, basil, tarragon, thyme, ginger, garlic, and shallot

Salads
Ambrosia, anise, caraway, chervil, chives, dandelion, fennel, leek, mint, garlic, mustard, oregano, parsley, peppers, rosemary, savory, shallot, basil, tarragon, and ginger

Eggs
Chives, cumin, leek, marjoram, oregano, parsley, peppers, tarragon, paprika, and shallot

Pickles
Coriander, mint, peppers, savory, shallot, and ginger

in an open plastic bag or at room temperature (if cool) in a small amount of water. It is best to find fresh herbs with their roots still intact since they will keep fresh and flavorful longer. Wrap the roots in a damp paper towel and cover with a plastic bag. Refrigerate, leaving the leaves out in the open. They can keep up to a week.

If you grow your own herbs, the best time to pick them is in the morning after the dew has evaporated. Do not wash until use. When using fresh herbs remember that they lose their flavor very quickly, so use them towards the end of cooking. Use dry herbs for long cooking and finish with fresh herbs for added flavor.

Using herbs and spices as an enhancement to a dish is one of the most important parts of great healthy cooking. But use them carefully. It is always easy to add but impossible to remove. Remember that you may have possible sensitivities or allergies to some herbs and spices. So be careful and keep notes in your journal and cooking recipes book.

Finally, here are examples of various herbs mixes that you can create at home.

Creole: 2 tsp. salt, 2 ½ Tbsp. paprika, 2 Tbsp. garlic powder, 1 Tbsp. dry oregano, 1 Tbsp. black pepper, 1 Tbsp. cayenne pepper, 1 Tbsp. onion powder, 1 Tbsp. dry thyme

Italian: 1 Tbsp. dry basil, 1/4 tsp. dry rosemary, ¼ tsp. dry thyme, ¼ tsp. dry marjoram, ¼ tsp. dry oregano, 1 Tbsp. dry parsley

Bouquet garni: 1 bay leaf, 3 sprigs fresh thyme, 4 sprigs fresh parsley, 1 garlic clove, 2 celery stalks, 2 pieces leek (green part only), 10 peppercorns

Fine herbs or salad herbs: 1 tsp. fresh chervil, 1 tsp. fresh chives, 1 tsp. fresh tarragon, 1 tsp. fresh parsley

Persillade: 2 large garlic cloves, ½ cup parsley, 3 Tbsp. shallots

Provence herbs: 1 Tbsp. dry thyme, 1 Tbsp. dry savory, 1 Tbsp. marjoram, 1 Tbsp. dry basil, 1 tsp. dry fennel, 1 Tbsp. dry rosemary, 2 dry bay leaf crumbled

Asian: 1 Tbsp. garlic powder, 1 Tbsp. ground ginger, 1/2 tsp. ground cumin, 1 tsp. coriander, 1 tsp. curry powder, ½ tsp. cayenne pepper, ½ tsp. dry mustard, 1/4 tsp. celery seeds, 1/4 tsp. nutmeg.

Part III

The Meals

Chapter 7

A Chef's Secrets for Easy, Quick Meals

Healthy Cooking Methods

Osteoporosis patients must **pay particular attention to the amount of fat used in cooking.** The use of Teflon pans helps in such cases. Limit the use of olive oil, canola oil, or grapeseed oil to a minimum. It is already done for you in these recipes. Use steaming, baking, grilling, broiling, or par-boiling methods as often as possible. For stir-fried and sautéing methods, using Teflon and very little oil is recommended. Brush the oil on the bottom of the pan or spray from your own pump spray bottle. Stay away from commercial oil spray that may contain fillers and other unhealthy ingredients. To thicken sauces, substitute arrowroot or cornstarch to the often found flour or beurre manié in recipes. There is no exact amount of thickening agent to give you, as the amount of arrowroot/cornstarch and water mixture may vary depending on the amount of water rendered by the ingredients involved or the reduction process. In these recipes, you will see cornstarch, but you can substitute arrowroot in the same way. A little secret to obtaining the right thickness for a sauce is to dip a spoon in the sauce, turn it over, and make a line across with your finger. Tilt over the spoon. If the sauce does not run over the line, it is the perfect thickness. If it does, you need to thicken with a little cornstarch-water mixture. Start with a spoon and see how it reacts after boiling. If it gets too thick, just add a little liquid to thin out.

Cooking Vegetables

When cooking vegetables, follow those basic directions:
* **For white vegetables** (onion, cauliflower, white cabbage, celery, cucumber, zucchini, etc.), use a little lemon juice or cream of tartar in the water to keep

them white. Do not use salt; they will turn yellowish.

- **For red vegetables** (example red cabbage), use an acid (vinegar) or cream of tartar to emphasize their red colors. Do not use salt; they will turn blue or blue-green.
- **For green vegetables** (broccoli, asparagus, green beans, etc.), use salt to emphasize a darker green color. Do not use acids or cream of tartar; they will turn olive green.
- **For yellow and orange vegetables or roots** (carrots, winter squash, sweet potatoes, tomatoes, red peppers, etc.), the use of acids or salt is not a problem.

Steam a variety of vegetables in one session. Once barely cooked, transfer them to an ice cold water bath to stop the cooking process. Pat dry and store separately in bags and place in the refrigerator. In a flash, you will be able to accompany a variety of dishes or snack on healthy foods. For a gourmet touch, drizzle a little bit of a prepared sauce (with your fish or chicken) over the vegetables and serve immediately. Remember lemon juice goes a long way and has no calories. Homemade tomato sauce is also a healthy choice, as it has the advantages of being low-fat and loaded with vitamins.

Remember, you do not have to eat only steamed or blanched vegetables to stay healthy. You can stir-fry them or sauté them with a little oil (1 teaspoon) once in a while and use different flavorings. The key is to avoid boredom and keep eating those vegetables. Blanched vegetables can be stored in the refrigerator 5 days without affecting them, and no longer than 7 days.

There are many ways to prepare and enjoy vegetables and there is no need to be concerned with loss of vitamins, as long as you do not overcook your vegetables. Keep them al dente and you will do a big favor to your body.

Some Tips for Saving Time

- Double the amount of food you prepare in one cooking session. Example: buy a couple of whole chickens and roast them in the oven while you are doing something else. Then divide them up for three different meals. For each meal, serve them with a different sauce and steamed, roasted, or stir-fried vegetables. Freeze or refrigerate in appropriate storage containers.
- Cook several skinless chicken breasts on an oiled baking sheet. Brush a little flavored oil and season to taste. Cook under the broiler until golden brown, turn over and brush with more flavored oil. Finish cooking until cooked through. The whole cooking process may take you 20 to 30 minutes depending upon the thickness of the breasts. Let cool, package individually, and store appropriately for later use.

- Do the same with fish fillets or steaks. The cooking process is much faster, so watch out. It will take a maximum 10 to 15 minutes. If the fillets have a skin on one side, place the skin side down on the baking sheet.

- Serve each meal with a different sauce, lemon or lime wedges, and steamed, roasted, or stir-fried vegetables (see below for suggestions). Freeze or refrigerate in appropriate storage containers.

- Wash and dry various greens. Store in plastic containers or bags for quick salads. Lettuces don't freeze well, so only prepare what you will eat within three or four days. It is ok to purchase pre-packaged and pre-cut organic mixed vegetables when time is of the essence during physically challenged days. Make sure you wash them before use.

- Make a week's worth of salad dressing and store in the refrigerator. Here is a recipe:

   ### Ingredients:
   1 tablespoon Dijon Mustard
   1 cup olive oil
   ½ cup walnut oil
   ½ cup wine vinegar
   1 shallot, minced
   2 garlic cloves, minced
   4 tablespoons freshly minced salad herbs
   Salt and pepper to taste

   ### Directions:
   Place all the ingredients in a tall container and season to taste. With a hand blender, mix well. Add a little water to thin out, if desired. Refrigerate for up to a week.

- Pre-cut large amount of vegetables and fruits. Store them in plastic containers or bags for quick snacks and side dishes. They can also be stored cooked (blanched or steamed and placed in ice cold water to stop the cooking, then pat dry before storing) in the refrigerator or freezer. Make sure you pack each vegetable separately to avoid the transfer of odors to other vegetables. Date before freezing. When things are tough, you may consider purchasing organic pre-cut vegetables to make it easier on you. Make sure you wash them before use to avoid possible illness and any preservatives that still may be on them to allow for longer storage.

- Shred low-fat cheese and store in plastic bags. This is also cheaper than buying cheese already shredded. Cheese does not freeze well. Remember a little freshly shredded Parmesan sprinkled at the last minute over a dish can do the trick without adding too much fat.

- Double recipes to start to build inventory in the freezer for days you are tired or last minute emergencies. Stock the freezer with freshly cooked vegetables, homemade soups, stews, purées, rice, etc.

- Prepare some healthy instant snacks and store individual portions for quick use.

- Make your own broth/stock and store in ice cube trays or small plastic bags for individual portions and in larger bags for bigger portions. When purchasing commercial broth/stock look for organic products that are low-sodium, and low-fat. If not organic, make sure they are free-range (for chicken), free of preservatives, gluten, additives, or artificial colorings.

- Finally, do not hesitate to recruit helpers for a cooking session together. This is a great deal of fun. Choose a day you feel well and people are available to come to your home. Together, you can prepare a couple of weeks worth of meals while enjoying each other's company. Children should also be involved, as it is good to spend the time together and you can teach them about responsibilities and living a healthy lifestyle. They will also learn about sharing, working with others, and helping others. One warning: Be very careful not to get hurt, as a crowded, busy kitchen may become a hazardous situation for you.

Chapter 8

The Recipes

About the Recipes

Because of their illness, many osteoporosis patients lose interest in food, which can have negative effects on their health. Consequently, **it is important to instill a passion for healthy and delicious foods** to awaken important senses and encourage patients to follow a healthier diet. The healthy recipes selected for this book may be quite a change for you. There is nothing wrong with treating yourself to something less healthy once in a while, even once a week, as long as you stay within your daily calories. Treating yourself will make it easier to maintain a healthier diet overall and will help you remain committed to your health and your happiness. Consider making small sacrifices by eating foods you don't particularly care for, but which you know agree with you, for the sake of your health. Eventually you will get used to these foods and, before you know it, you won't even think about it. After all, a healthy diet is all about balance.

Many of these recipes include fresh ingredients. Occasionally commercial products may be called for, but try to keep these to a minimum and purchase organic products instead. Though some of the recipes might appear challenging, they are all really simple. Once you practice the healthy cooking techniques a few times, they will become easy. Don't let anyone discourage you in your attempt to learn new healthy cooking techniques and eat right. Perhaps they don't cook, don't know how, find cooking a waste of time, or not worth the effort. Show them how easy it is and how pleasurable it is to prepare and eat natural, healthy foods.

Finally, **do not be afraid to substitute ingredients in these recipes to meet your personal needs.** Recipes are meant to be changed. In fact, always consider a recipe book as a base or guideline for you, the cook. Bringing your own touch, knowing what you or your family likes, is what will make regular meals become extraordinary meals. So if you do not like Ahi, feel free to substitute another fish which has similar nutrients and that agrees with you. If you don't like the herbs, consult the list for guidelines and substitute herbs that you know you will enjoy. Be adventurous and experience the joy of cooking and eating healthy foods.

Breakfast

With the hectic pace of life today, spending a few minutes sitting down to eat breakfast seems the least of many people's concerns. This is a huge mistake. If you don't take the time to eat first thing in the morning, you will throw off your eating regimen for the rest of the day. **You don't have to indulge in a huge breakfast to give your body what it needs to get moving.** Organic cereals listed in the recipes are a quick and easy way to start your day, and they will give you a start on your needed calcium intake. When you have energy, enjoy a more complex breakfast recipe such as cheese blintzes. When preparing eggs, purchase organic or free-range eggs with Omega-3 fatty acids, which will provide you with healthier and more anti-inflammatory sources than regular eggs. Don't forget to hydrate with water, freshly squeezed juice, a homemade smoothie, or tea.

The following recipes are designed to jump-start your day and provide you with the physical and mental energy you will need to get through the morning. Over time you will notice that the first part of your day is a lot easier to handle when you provide your body with the nutrients it needs. Your energy boost is sure to increase your productivity—and encourage your metabolism to function better.

Granola with Raisins and Dates

serves 1

✓ *Option:*
Add 1 tablespoon
of flaxseeds

ingredients

1/2 cup granola
1/2 cup low-fat milk
1/4 medium apple, diced
1 teaspoon walnuts, chopped
1 date, chopped

cooking instructions

Mix the granola with the milk. Add the apple, walnuts, date, and serve immediately.

nutritional facts

Per Serving: 365 Cal (16% from Fat, 10% from Protein, 74% from Carb); 9 g Protein; 7 g Tot Fat; 2 g Sat Fat; 2 g Mono Fat; 71 g Carb; 6 g Fiber; 40 g Sugar; 184 mg Calcium; 2 mg Iron; 185 mg Sodium; 10 mg Cholesterol

Cream of Millet

serves 1

ingredients

1/4 cup pearl millet
3/4 cup to 1cup low-fat almond milk
1 teaspoon pumpkin pie spices
(optional)
1/2 peach, peeled and diced
2 teaspoons maple syrup
2 teaspoons slivered almonds
1 teaspoon flaxseed oil
Small pinch of salt

✔ *You may substitute low-fat almond milk with low-fat rice milk, low-fat soy milk, or low-fat milk and flaxseed oil with ground flaxseeds (up to 1 tablespoon). Feel free to exchange the peach for apricot, apple, mango, or berries.*

cooking instructions

Warm the 1 cup of milk, salt, and the spices over medium heat. Wash the millet a couple of times and drain well. Place the millet in a pan. Add the almonds and the warm flavored milk. Reduce heat and simmer for 20 minutes or until the liquid is absorbed.

Transfer to a serving bowl and mix in the maple syrup. Top with the fruits, drizzle with flaxseed oil, and serve immediately. When using less cooking liquid, the grain is fluffier and crunchier. Using more liquid will create a more moist, soft texture. This is about personal preferences, so experiment and find the texture you like.

nutritional facts

Per Serving: 384 Cal (19% from Fat, 15% from Protein, 65% from Carb); 15 g Protein; 8 g Tot Fat; 1 g Sat Fat; 2 g Mono Fat; 63 g Carb; 5 g Fiber; 25 g Sugar; 525 mg Calcium; 2 mg Iron; 132 mg Sodium; 5 mg Cholesterol

Muesli with Peach and Almonds

serves 1

✓ *Option:*
Add 1 tablespoon of flaxseeds

ingredients

1/2 cup Muesli cereal
1/2 cup low-fat yogurt
2 teaspoons almonds, slivered or sliced
1 small peach
Low-fat milk

cooking instructions

In a bowl mix the cereal with the yogurt. Thin out with a little milk. Top with the peaches, almonds, and serve immediately.

nutritional facts

Per Serving: 211 Cal (29% from Fat, 27% from Protein, 44% from Carb); 15 g Protein; 7 g Tot Fat; 3 g Sat Fat; 3 g Mono Fat; 24 g Carb; 2 g Fiber; 22 g Sugar; 467 mg Calcium; 1 mg Iron; 172 mg Sodium; 15 mg Cholesterol

Oatmeal with Kiwi and Banana

Option:
Add 1 teaspoon
flaxseed

serves 1

ingredients

1/2 cup oatmeal
1 cup low-fat milk, hot 1 teaspoon
almonds
1 kiwi, diced
1/2 banana, diced

cooking instructions

Mix the oatmeal with the hot milk until the liquid is incorporated. Add in the almonds, kiwi, banana, and serve immediately.

nutritional facts

Per Serving: 389 Cal (16% from Fat, 14% from Protein, 69% from Carb); 15 g Protein; 8 g Tot Fat; 3 g Sat Fat; 2 g Mono Fat; 72 g Carb; 10 g Fiber; 30 g Sugar; 339 mg Calcium; 2 mg Iron; 105 mg Sodium; 20 mg Cholesterol

Orange Wheat Muffins with Cream Cheese

serves 12

> ✓ *You may substitute 2 eggs with 4 egg whites. Careful, this recipe can be quite laxative. Muffin freezes very well when wrapped individually in plastic and placed in a freezer bag.*

ingredients

1 cup unbleached all-purpose flour
1/2 cup whole wheat flour
1/2 cup flaxseed meal
1/3 cup honey
1 teaspoon baking soda
1 tablespoon baking powder
1/4 teaspoon salt
1 teaspoon orange extract
1 teaspoon orange zest

2 large eggs
2 tablespoons canola oil
1/2 cup pumpkin puree (organic can)
1 cup plain low-fat yogurt
12 tablespoons low-fat cream cheese
12 teaspoons pumpkin seeds
Pumpkin pie spices or cinnamon to taste (optional)

cooking instructions

Preheat the oven to 375° F.

Blend the flours, flaxseed meal, honey, baking soda, baking powder, and salt in a mixing bowl. Blend in the orange extract, orange zest, canola oil, eggs, pumpkin puree, yogurt, and mix well. Fill muffin pan and bake for 25 minutes or until cooked through and golden brown.

Top each muffin with 1 tablespoon of low-fat cream cheese. Sprinkle spices or cinnamon, pumpkin seeds, and serve immediately.

nutritional facts

Per Serving: 193 Cal (31% from Fat, 14% from Protein, 56% from Carb); 7 g Protein; 7 g Tot Fat; 2 g Sat Fat; 3 g Mono Fat; 27 g Carb; 2 g Fiber; 10 g Sugar; 136 mg Calcium; 2 mg Iron; 350 mg Sodium; 51 mg Cholesterol

Acai and Soy Milk Smoothie

serves 2

ingredients

4 ounces pure Acai,
no sugar added
1 large banana, skin removed
1 apple; skin removed, cored,
and chopped
2 oranges, juiced
8 ounces low-fat soy milk
(or low-fat milk)
1 tablespoon flaxseeds
3 tablespoons powdered
low-fat milk
Ice

✔ *Option: Add up to 1 tablespoon of flaxseeds*

Acai is a fruit grown in the Amazon rain forest. It has a berry chocolate-like flavor and is considered one of nature's healthiest foods. Its high amounts of antioxidants, anthocyanins (approximately 20 times the amount in red wine), amino acids, essential omegas, fibers and protein make Acai a great treat to a healthy diet.

If not available in your local stores, check the internet as various sites do sell this product. You may substitute Acai with Noni or Gac juice.

cooking instructions

Place all the ingredients in a blender. Add ice to almost fill the container, and puree on high speed. Divide between two tall glasses and serve immediately.

nutritional facts

Per Serving: 270 Cal (19% from Fat, 12% from Protein, 69% from Carb); 9 g Protein; 6 g Tot Fat; 1 g Sat Fat; 0 g Mono Fat; 51 g Carb; 8 g Fiber; 33 g Sugar; 162 mg Calcium; 1 mg Iron; 55 mg Sodium; 1 mg Cholesterol

Scrambled Eggs with Mushrooms and Onions

serves 2

ingredients

1 teaspoon olive oil
1/2 small yellow onion, chopped
(about 2 ounces)
4 white mushrooms, sliced
(about 4 ounces)

1 garlic clove, minced
1 tablespoon freshly minced basil
4 eggs
1 tablespoon low-fat milk
Salt and pepper to taste

cooking instructions

Heat the oil in a nonstick pan over medium heat. Add the onion and sauté until translucent. Add the garlic, mushrooms, and sauté until mushrooms are cooked through. Beat the eggs with the milk in a bowl. Add the basil and season to taste. Pour the mixture over the vegetables. Cook over medium heat, stirring and scraping the bottom and sides of the pan constantly with a wooden spoon. As soon as the eggs begin to set, remove from heat, continue to stir for a few seconds, and serve immediately.

nutritional facts

Per Serving: 240 Cal (53% from Fat, 29% from Protein, 18% from Carb); 18 g Protein; 14 g Tot Fat; 4 g Sat Fat; 6 g Mono Fat; 11 g Carb; 1 g Fiber; 4 g Sugar; 106 mg Calcium; 3 mg Iron; 171 mg Sodium; 491 mg Cholesterol

Salmon and Asparagus Omelet

serves 2

ingredients

4 eggs
1 teaspoon canola oil
1/2 tablespoon water
3 ounces wild smoked salmon
4 asparagus spears, cooked
1/4 small onion, diced
(about 1 ounce)

1/2 small garlic clove, minced
A couple pinches of fresh dill, minced
Lemon juice to taste
Salt and pepper to taste

cooking instructions

Heat the oil in a nonstick pan over medium heat. Add the onions and sauté until translucent. Add the garlic, asparagus, lemon juice, and sauté for 2 minutes. Spread the vegetables evenly over the bottom of the pan.

In a bowl, beat the eggs, water, and season to taste. Add the egg mixture to the asparagus and let the eggs set. Add the smoked salmon and sprinkle the dill. Reduce heat and continue to cook for 2 to 3 minutes. Fold over in half, cook another minute, and serve immediately.

nutritional facts

Per Serving: 260 Cal (56% from Fat, 38% from Protein, 6% from Carb); 24 g Protein; 16 g Tot Fat; 4 g Sat Fat; 7 g Mono Fat; 4 g Carb; 1 g Fiber; 2 g Sugar; 97 mg Calcium; 4 mg Iron; 503 mg Sodium; 501 mg Cholesterol

French Toast with Orange Slices

serves 4

✓ *For variety you may flavor with cinnamon and nutmeg.*

ingredients

3 eggs
2/3 cup low-fat milk
1 ½ teaspoon orange extract
Pinch salt
8 slices whole wheat bread
Vegetable oil
4 tablespoons maple syrup
2 oranges, peeled and sliced

cooking instructions

Beat together the eggs, milk, orange extract, and salt. Dip the bread slices in the mixture. Soak them well.

Preheat two large skillets or a griddle with a little vegetable oil. Add the bread slices and brown on both sides. Serve immediately with maple syrup and orange slices.

nutritional facts

Per Serving: 351 Cal (17% from Fat, 14% from Protein, 68% from Carb); 13 g Protein; 7 g Tot Fat; 2 g Sat Fat; 3 g Mono Fat; 60 g Carb; 4 g Fiber; 22 g Sugar; 166 mg Calcium; 3 mg Iron; 463 mg Sodium; 167 mg Cholesterol

Cheese Blintzes with Raspberries

serves 4

ingredients

For the crêpes:
1 cup sifted flour
2 extra-large eggs, beaten
1 tablespoon honey, warmed in the microwave
2 tablespoons unsalted butter, melted

Pinch of salt
1 cup low-fat milk
2 cups fresh raspberries

For the filling:
1 ½ cup low-fat cottage cheese
1/4 cup low-fat sour cream
1 tablespoon honey, warmed up in the microwave
Pinch of salt

cooking instructions

For the filling: Mix in a bowl the cottage cheese, sour cream, honey, and salt. Refrigerate until use.

Place 1 cup of the raspberries in a blender and reduce to a sauce. Pass through a sieve to remove seeds and refrigerate until use.

For the crêpes: Place the flour in a bowl. Blend in the eggs, honey, salt, and melted butter. Slowly whisk in the milk. Let the batter rest for 30 minutes. Before use, add a little water to thin out the batter.

Heat a nonstick pan or crêpe pan over medium heat. Soak a small piece of paper towel in vegetable oil and swirl quickly over the pan. Add enough batter and swirl to cover the entire bottom. Cook until golden brown and remove from heat. Do not cook the other side. Repeat until all the batter has been used.

Place the golden brown side of the crêpes side up. Divide the filling among the center length of the crêpes. Roll a bit, tuck both edges, and finish rolling to retain all the filling inside the crêpes. Cook the crêpes over medium heat in a greased skillet until golden brown on all sides. Serve immediately with the raspberry coulis and the remaining raspberries.

nutritional facts

Per Serving (2 crêpes): 419 Cal (35% from Fat, 21% from Protein, 44% from Carb); 22 g Protein; 16 g Tot Fat; 9 g Sat Fat; 5 g Mono Fat; 47 g Carb; 5 g Fiber; 15 g Sugar; 181 mg Calcium; 3 mg Iron; 419 mg Sodium; 163 mg Cholesterol

Soup & Salad

Soups and salads are very versatile and can be served as an appetizer, main course, side dish, or even dessert. **They are quick and healthy meal options, and can be a great way to use leftovers.** In addition, salad recipes don't require much cooking, if any, and the techniques used are very basic. Salads taste better when put together at the last minute. They will be more appealing and pleasing with their fresh colors, textures, and flavors.

Here are a few important things to keep in mind whenever you prepare soups or salads.

First, stay away from croutons and avoid unhealthy salad dressings. Healthy dressing choices include oil (particularly olive oil, canola oil, avocado oil, flaxseed oil, and/or walnut oil unless you have a nut allergy, and vinegar (wine, balsamic, or apple) or citrus juices with fresh herbs. Apple cider vinegar can be beneficial to your health due to its cleansing and healing properties. So don't hesitate to substitute it for vinegar or citrus juice.

If you have no problems with nuts, use a few nuts in your salads such as walnuts, almonds, pistachios, hazelnuts, and pepitas, or sprinkle freshly ground flaxseeds. Include lots of vegetables in your salads, particularly the recommended greens and vegetables in the shopping list of this book, as they are very powerful antioxidants. **Onions, scallions, shallots, and garlic are also important, as they too have cancer-fighting properties and help lower bad cholesterol (LDL).**

Your salads may contain an adequate amount of protein, which should come from lean sources such as fish, poultry, or tofu. **Plant protein sources such as dry beans, lentils, and garbanzos may be substituted.** They will provide fibers and polyphenols which have good anti-inflammatory and anti-allergenic properties. Note: if you are not a vegetarian, try to maintain a good mix of animal and plant proteins to ensure you get the nutrients you need. **The addition of fresh herbs and freshly ground spices will add flavors and antioxidants which will help boost your immune system.** Limit cheeses to lower-fat brands to minimize fat intake. Shredding just a little fresh parmesan over a salad can add much flavor without adding unwanted calories. As for a soup, be careful not to overcook the vegetables you add to your soup bases, as they will lose their nutrients. This can be tricky because a soup's ingredients will continue to cook as long as the soup is hot, even after you've taken it off the stove. So undercook the vegetables to allow for that extra time and to preserve their nutritive values. For herbs in soup, use dry herbs at first and finish with fresh herbs (using fresh herbs at the beginning will only be a waste of money, as the flavors will evaporate during the cooking process.) For balanced nutrition, be sure to include lean proteins, complex carbohydrates, and vegetables just as you would in your salads.

Broccoli Soup

serves 4

ingredients

2 teaspoons grapeseed oil
1 small onion, diced
(about 4 ounces)
4 large broccoli heads, chopped
(about 2 pounds)
1 garlic clove, minced
3 cups chicken or vegetable stock
(low-fat and low-sodium)
1 bouquet garni
2 to 3 tablespoons cornstarch
mixed with a little water
1 cup low-fat milk
Salt and pepper

cooking instructions

Heat the oil in a large pan over high heat. Add the onion and sauté until translucent. Add 3/4 of the broccoli, garlic, stock, bouquet garni, and bring to a boil. Reduce heat and simmer until the broccoli is very tender. Remove the bouquet garni and puree with a hand blender. Add the milk and bring back to a boil. Thicken with arrowroot/cornstarch water mixture, a little at a time, until you reach the desired consistency. Add the remaining broccoli and bring to a boil. Cook until tender, adjust seasonings, and serve immediately.

nutritional facts

Per Serving: 178 Cal (20% from Fat, 24% from Protein, 56% from Carb); 12 g Protein; 4 g Tot Fat; 1 g Sat Fat; 1 g Mono Fat; 27 g Carb; 6 g Fiber; 8 g Sugar; 212 mg Calcium; 2 mg Iron; 518 mg Sodium; 5 mg Cholesterol

French Onion Soup

serves 4

ingredients

2 tablespoons grapeseed oil
3 large onions, thinly sliced
(about 1 ½ pounds)
2 tablespoons Cognac (optional)
2 tablespoons flour
6 to 7 cups beef stock (low-fat and
low-sodium)

3/4 cup Swiss cheese or Gruyère,
shredded (about 6 ounces)
Salt and pepper to taste

cooking instructions

Heat the oil in a large pan over medium heat. Add the onions and
cook until golden brown. Stir occasionally to avoid burning. This
will take up to 20 minutes. Carefully add the cognac and flambé
(optional). Sprinkle with the flour and mix well. Add the beef stock
and bring to a boil over
high heat. Reduce heat and
simmer for 20 to 25 minutes.
Skim any foam or fat that
may rise to the surface.
Adjust seasonings and serve
immediately with the cheese.

nutritional facts

Per Serving: 232 Cal (52% from Fat,
21% from Protein, 27% from Carb);
12 g Protein; 13 g Tot Fat; 6 g Sat
Fat; 3 g Mono Fat; 15 g Carb;
2 g Fiber; 5 g Sugar; 264 mg Calcium; 1 mg Iron; 840 mg Sodium;
26 mg Cholesterol

Oysters Stew

serves 4

ingredients

2 cups low-fat milk
1/2 tablespoon olive oil
1/2 quart oysters
1 tablespoon parsley
Salt and pepper to taste
Cornstarch mixed with a little
water

cooking instructions

Scald the milk in a saucepan over medium heat. Thicken with a little cornstarch to obtain a sauce consistency. Carefully open the oysters and transfer their liquid to a bowl. Remove flesh and add to a pan. Add the olive oil and quickly sauté under medium heat. Add the liquid and simmer (do not boil) until the edges begin to curl. Add the hot milk, parsley, and season to taste. Bring to a simmer (do not boil) and serve immediately.

nutritional facts

Per Serving: 167 Cal (39% from Fat, 32% from Protein, 29% from Carb); 13 g Protein; 7 g Tot Fat; 3 g Sat Fat; 1 g Mono Fat; 12 g Carb; 0 g Fiber; 6 g Sugar; 201 mg Calcium; 8 mg Iron; 607 mg Sodium; 75 mg Cholesterol

Lentil Soup with Ground Turkey

serves 4

ingredients

3 teaspoons canola oil
1 large onion, diced small
(about 8 ounces)
1 large carrot, diced small (about
4 ounces)
2 large celery stalks, diced small
(about 4 ounces)
2 garlic cloves, minced

6 cups chicken stock
(low-fat and low-sodium)
3 cups dried lentils
8 ounces ground turkey
1 bouquet garni
Salt and pepper

cooking instructions

Heat 2 teaspoons of oil in a large pan over high heat. Add the onion and sauté until translucent. Add the carrot, celery, garlic, and cook for 2 minutes. Add the stock, lentils, bouquet garni, and bring to a boil. Reduce heat, cover, and simmer for 35 minutes. Skim the surface as needed. Continue to simmer uncovered for 10 minutes in order to thicken the soup. Remove the bouquet garni. Heat 1 teaspoon of oil in a medium pan over high heat. Add the ground turkey and sauté until cooked through (about 3 to 4 minutes). Strain and disregard any fat. Add the meat to the prepared lentils and bring to a boil. Adjust seasonings and serve immediately.

If the soup turns out too thick, adjust with stock. If the soup is too thin, reduce the liquid more or mash a little bit of the lentils and return mixture to the pan.

nutritional facts

Per Serving: 262 Cal (19% from Fat, 39% from Protein, 42% from Carb); 26 g Protein; 6 g Tot Fat; 1 g Sat Fat; 2 g Mono Fat; 28 g Carb; 9 g Fiber; 6 g Sugar; 87 mg Calcium; 5 mg Iron; 617 mg Sodium; 37 mg Cholesterol

Mushroom and Barley Soup

serves 4

ingredients

2 teaspoons grapeseed oil
1/3 cup barley (about 2 ounces)
1 small onion, diced
(about 4 ounces)
1 large carrot, diced
(about 4 ounces)
1 small turnip, diced
(about 4 ounces)
4 cups chicken or vegetable stock
(low-fat and low-sodium)

1 bouquet garni
8 ounces mushrooms, peeled and
diced
1 cup low-fat milk
2 tablespoons minced parsley
Salt and pepper

cooking instructions

Cook the barley according to package directions. Drain and set aside.

Heat the oil in a pan over high heat. Add the onion, carrot, turnip, and sauté for 2 minutes. Add the stock, bouquet garni, and bring to a boil. Reduce heat and simmer until the vegetables are barely tender. Add the mushrooms, drained barley, milk, and bring to a simmer. Continue to cook for 3 to 5 minutes. Add parsley, adjust seasonings, and serve immediately.

nutritional facts

Per Serving: 186 Cal (19% from Fat, 20% from Protein, 60% from Carb); 10 g Protein; 4 g Tot Fat; 1 g Sat Fat; 1 g Mono Fat; 29 g Carb; 7 g Fiber; 9 g Sugar; 130 mg Calcium; 2 mg Iron; 609 mg Sodium; 5 mg Cholesterol

Roasted Red Vegetables and Feta Soup

serves 4

ingredients

2 teaspoons olive oil
5 large tomatoes, halved length-wise (about 2 pounds)
3 large red bell peppers, seeded and quartered (about 1 1/2 pounds)
4 garlic cloves, peeled

1 teaspoon freshly minced thyme
2 tablespoons freshly minced basil
2 cups vegetables stock (low-fat and low-sodium)
4 tablespoons feta cheese, crumbled

cooking instructions

Preheat the oven to 450°F. Place the tomatoes, red bell peppers, and garlic on an oiled cookie sheet. Drizzle a little olive oil over the vegetables and roast for 30 minutes or until brown. Remove from the oven and cool.

Puree the vegetables in a blender. Transfer to a saucepan; add the thyme, and enough stock to bring to a soup consistency. Add the basil, bring to a boil over medium heat, and adjust seasoning. Serve immediately with the crumbled feta cheese.

nutritional facts

Per Serving: 198 Cal (28% from Fat, 13% from Protein, 59% from Carb); 7 g Protein; 7 g Tot Fat; 2 g Sat Fat; 3 g Mono Fat; 32 g Carb; 7 g Fiber; 15 g Sugar; 177 mg Calcium; 4 mg Iron; 194 mg Sodium; 8 mg Cholesterol

Potato and Watercress Soup

serves 4

> ✔ *This soup can also be served cold.*
> *You may substitute leek (white part only) for the onion.*

ingredients

1 teaspoon grapeseed oil
2 medium potatoes, peeled and thinly sliced (about 1 cup)
1 small onion, diced (about 1/4 cup)
1 garlic clove, minced
2 ½ cups vegetable stock (low-fat and low-sodium)

1/2 cup low-fat milk
1 bunch watercress (about 1 cup)
1 bouquet garni
2 tablespoons minced parsley
Salt and pepper to taste

cooking instructions

Heat the oil in a saucepan over high heat. Add the onion and sauté until translucent. Add the potatoes, garlic, stock, watercress, bouquet garni, and bring to boil. Reduce heat and simmer for 20 minutes. Remove bouquet garni and purée with a hand blender or a food mill. Add the milk, parsley, and bring to boil. Season to taste and serve immediately.

nutritional facts

Per Serving: 106 Cal (18% from Fat, 13% from Protein, 69% from Carb); 4 g Protein; 2 g Tot Fat; 1 g Sat Fat; 0 g Mono Fat; 19 g Carb; 1 g Fiber; 4 g Sugar; 96 mg Calcium; 1 mg Iron; 102 mg Sodium; 2 mg Cholesterol

Cod and Corn Chowder

serves 4

ingredients

2 teaspoons grapeseed oil
1 medium onion, diced (about 6 ounces)
1 medium carrot, diced (about 3 ounces)
1 large celery stalk, diced (about 2 ounces)
2 medium potatoes, peeled and diced (about 12 ounces)

Corn kernels from 2 corn ears
2 cups vegetable stock (low-fat and low-sodium)
1 cup low-fat milk
1 pound cod fish fillets, diced
2 tablespoons freshly minced parsley
Salt and pepper to taste

cooking instructions

Heat the oil in a saucepan over high heat. Add the onion and sauté until translucent. Add the carrot, celery, potatoes, stock, and bring to a boil. Reduce heat and simmer for 15 minutes. Mash the potato with a fork and continue to reduce until you obtain a creamy texture. Add the corn, milk, fish, parsley, and bring to a boil. Continue to simmer for another 5 minutes. Adjust seasoning and serve immediately.

nutritional facts

Per Serving: 236 Cal (17% from Fat, 26% from Protein, 57% from Carb); 16 g Protein; 5 g Tot Fat; 1 g Sat Fat; 1 g Mono Fat; 35 g Carb; 4 g Fiber; 9 g Sugar; 138 mg Calcium; 1 mg Iron; 159 mg Sodium; 30 mg Cholesterol

Chickpea, Tomato, and Rice Soup

serves 4

ingredients

1 teaspoon olive oil
1 small onion, diced
(about 4 ounces)
8 ounces chopped Italian plum
tomatoes (can)
1/2 cup brown rice
12 ounces cooked chickpeas
3 garlic cloves, minced

5 cups chicken stock
1/2 teaspoon fresh rosemary,
minced
2 tablespoons fresh parsley,
chopped
Salt and pepper to taste

cooking instructions

Heat the oil in a large pan over high heat. Add the onion and sauté until translucent. Add the garlic, tomatoes, rosemary, and cook until the juices are evaporated. Add the rice, stock, and bring to boil. Reduce heat, cover, and simmer for 25 minutes. Add the chickpeas and continue to cook for 5 minutes, or until the rice is cooked through. Add the parsley, season to taste, and serve immediately.

nutritional facts

Per Serving: 391 Cal (15% from Fat, 22% from Protein, 64% from Carb); 22 g Protein; 6 g Tot Fat; 1 g Sat Fat; 2 g Mono Fat; 64 g Carb; 16 g Fiber; 12 g Sugar; 136 mg Calcium; 7 mg Iron; 719 mg Sodium; 0 mg Cholesterol

White Beans Stew

serves 4

ingredients

1 teaspoon olive oil
1 pound dried white beans
1 small onion, diced
(about 4 ounces)
1 medium carrot, diced
(about 3 ounces)
1 large celery stalk, diced
(about 2 ounces)
1 tablespoons garlic cloves,
minced

7 ounces canned tomato purée
(preferably organic)
2 teaspoons flour
1 tablespoons fresh parsley,
minced
1 bouquet garni
2 1/4 cups chicken stock
(low-fat and low-sodium)
Salt and pepper to taste

cooking instructions

Soak the beans overnight. Discard the water.

Place the beans in a large pan and add enough water to cover them. Bring to a boil over high heat. Remove from heat and let stand covered for 5 minutes. Drain the beans and rinse under cold water.

Heat the oil in a large pan over high heat. Add the onions, carrots, celery, garlic, and sauté for 2 minutes. Mix in the flour. Add the beans, bouquet garni, and 4 cups of stock. If the beans are not covered, add more water. Bring to a boil. Cover, reduce heat, and simmer for 30 minutes or until tender. Add the tomato purée and bring to a boil. Add parsley and season to taste. If the mixture is too thin, remove some beans, mash them, and add them back to the stew. Serve immediately.

nutritional facts

Per Serving: 461 Cal (5% from Fat, 24% from Protein, 71% from Carb); 29 g Protein; 3 g Tot Fat; 1 g Sat Fat; 1 g Mono Fat; 84 g Carb; 19 g Fiber; 8 g Sugar; 310 mg Calcium; 14 mg Iron; 461 mg Sodium; 1 mg Cholesterol

Pumpkin Soup and Pepitas

serves 4

ingredients

1 teaspoon olive oil
1 medium onion, minced
(about 6 ounces)
2 garlic cloves, minced
3 cups chicken stock
(low-fat and low-sodium)
One 15-ounce can unflavored
pumpkin puree

1 ½ cup low-fat evaporated milk
1 teaspoon vanilla
2 fresh sage leaves
2 tablespoons pepitas
Salt and pepper to taste

cooking instructions

Heat the oil in a large pan over medium heat. Add the onions and sauté until translucent. Stir in the garlic and continue to cook for another minute. Add the pumpkin purée, stock, and sage. Mix occasionally while bringing to a boil. Add the evaporated milk, vanilla, and bring to a boil still stirring occasionally. Season to taste and garnish with the pepitas before serving.

nutritional facts

Per Serving: 178 Cal (22% from Fat, 19% from Protein, 59% from Carb); 9 g Protein; 4 g Tot Fat; 1 g Sat Fat; 2 g Mono Fat; 27 g Carb; 4 g Fiber; 15 g Sugar; 267 mg Calcium; 2 mg Iron; 587 mg Sodium; 3 mg Cholesterol

Smoked Salmon, Potato, and Watercress Salad

serves 4

ingredients

12 ounces smoked salmon, diced

3 cooked potatoes, sliced (about 1 pound)

1 bunch watercress

1 cup cooked broccoli

1 hardboiled egg, chopped (or 2 egg whites for less cholesterol)

2 tablespoons white wine vinegar

4 tablespoons olive oil

1 teaspoon Dijon mustard

1 tablespoon minced shallots

2 tablespoons minced salad herb

Salt and pepper to taste

cooking instructions

Mix the vinegar, mustard, and shallots in a bowl. Whisk in the olive oil, 1 tablespoon of minced herbs, and season to taste.

Mix half of the dressing with the potatoes. Mix the remaining dressing with the watercress. Divide the watercress among four plates. Top with the potatoes, broccoli, and salmon. Sprinkle with the chopped egg, remaining minced herbs, and serve immediately.

nutritional facts

Per Serving: 377 Cal (48% from Fat, 22% from Protein, 30% from Carb); 21 g Protein; 20 g Tot Fat; 3 g Sat Fat; 12 g Mono Fat; 28 g Carb; 3 g Fiber; 2 g Sugar; 46 mg Calcium; 2 mg Iron; 80 mg Sodium; 83 mg Cholesterol

Greens with Goat Cheese, Dates, and Walnuts

serves 4

ingredients

5 ounces mesclun
4 ounces goat cheese
1/4 cup walnuts, chopped
8 Medjool dates
1 teaspoon Dijon mustard
1 large garlic clove, minced
1 large shallot, minced

2 tablespoons apple cider vinegar
2 tablespoons olive oil
2 tablespoons walnut oil
2 tablespoons salad herbs
Salt and pepper to taste

cooking instructions

In a bowl mix the mustard, garlic, shallot, and vinegar. Whisk in the oils, herbs, and season to taste.

Place the mesclun in a bowl and mix in 3/4 of the vinaigrette. Crumble the goat cheese over the greens. Add the walnuts and dates. Drizzle the remaining dressing and serve immediately.

nutritional facts

Per Serving: 384 Cal (54% from Fat, 8% from Protein, 38% from Carb); 8 g Protein; 24 g Tot Fat; 7 g Sat Fat; 10 g Mono Fat; 39 g Carb; 4 g Fiber; 33 g Sugar; 97 mg Calcium; 2 mg Iron; 122 mg Sodium; 13 mg Cholesterol

Tomato, Mozzarella, and Basil Salad

serves 4

ingredients

6 large tomatoes, sliced
(about 2 1/4 pounds)
1 shallot, minced
1 garlic clove, minced
4 tablespoons olive oil
2 tablespoons white wine or apple
cider vinegar

8 fresh basil leaves
8 ounces fresh mozzarella cheese,
sliced

cooking instructions

Spread the tomatoes over a large platter. Sprinkle with salt and set aside for 20 minutes. Mince half the basil leaves and set aside. Shred the remaining leaves and set aside.

Mix the shallot, garlic, and vinegar in a bowl. Whisk in the oil, the minced basil, and season to taste.

Transfer the tomatoes to another serving platter. Alternate a tomato slice and mozzarella slice. Spread the shredded basil, pour the dressing over, and serve immediately.

nutritional facts

Per Serving: 316 Cal (64% from Fat, 19% from Protein, 16% from Carb); 16 g Protein; 23 g Tot Fat; 8 g Sat Fat; 11 g Mono Fat; 13 g Carb; 3 g Fiber; 1 g Sugar; 460 mg Calcium; 1 mg Iron; 373 mg Sodium; 36 mg Cholesterol

Salmon and Asparagus Salad

serves 4

ingredients

5 ounces salad greens
16 asparagus stalks
1 large bulb fennel, sliced thinly
(about 12 ounces)
4 four-ounce salmon fillets
1 teaspoon Dijon mustard
2 tablespoons orange juice

1 teaspoon orange zest
4 tablespoons olive oil
1 tablespoon salad herbs, minced
1 orange, peeled and sliced
Salt and pepper

cooking instructions

In a bowl mix the mustard, juice, oil, zest, herbs, and season to taste.

Preheat a steamer. Trim the asparagus and place them in the steamer basket. Cook until barely tender. Transfer the asparagus to a platter and let cool.

Season the salmon fillets and add to the steamer basket. Top with the fennel slices and steam until cooked through, about 10 to 12 minutes. Time may vary based on the thickness of the fillets.

Mix the dressing with the greens. Divide equally among four plates. Top with the fillets, fennel, asparagus, orange slices, and serve immediately.

nutritional facts

Per Serving: 343 Cal (52% from Fat, 31% from Protein, 17% from Carb); 27 g Protein; 20 g Tot Fat; 4 g Sat Fat; 12 g Mono Fat; 15 g Carb; 5 g Fiber; 5 g Sugar; 367 mg Calcium; 3 mg Iron; 156 mg Sodium; 44 mg Cholesterol

Seared Ahi Salad

serves 2

ingredients

4 four-ounce Ahi fillets,
Sushi grade
4 ounces mixed greens
12 cherry tomatoes
(about 6 ounces)
4 white mushrooms, sliced (about
4 ounces)
1 large carrot, sliced diagonally
(about 4 ounces)
2 cups broccoli (about 6 ounces)

2 ounces sugar snap peas
1 teaspoon sesame oil
1 teaspoon soy sauce
1 tablespoon lime juice
4 teaspoons olive oil
1 teaspoon ginger, minced
4 teaspoons sesame seeds
1 lime
Salt and pepper to taste

cooking instructions

Mix the sesame oil, soy sauce, lime juice, 1 tablespoon olive oil, and ginger in a bowl. Season with pepper and set aside.

Par-boil the carrot, broccoli, and sugar snap peas to desired tenderness. Transfer to an ice-cold water bath to stop the cooking process. Pat dry and set aside.

Mix the greens with the prepared dressing and equally divide among four plates. Top with the carrot slices, mushrooms, sugar snap peas, and set aside.

Preheat 1 teaspoon olive oil in a nonstick pan over high heat. Season the fish with pepper and a little salt. Sear the fish for 2 minutes on each side. You may sear longer, if you want the center of the fish more cooked.

Slice the fish and spread over the top of the prepared salad. Sprinkle withwith the sesame seeds and serve immediately with lime wedges.

nutritional facts

Per Serving: 296 Cal (40% from Fat, 41% from Protein, 19% from Carb); 31 g Protein; 13 g Tot Fat; 2 g Sat Fat; 6 g Mono Fat; 15 g Carb; 5 g Fiber; 4 g Sugar; 88 mg Calcium; 3 mg Iron; 159 mg Sodium; 43 mg Cholesterol

Chicken Salad with Fruit

serves 4

ingredients

5 ounces fresh mixed greens
12 ounces cooked chicken breasts
(without skin), diced
1 avocado, diced
1 large apple, diced
(about 6 ounces)
1 orange, peeled and wedged
(about 6 ounces)
2 kiwis, peeled and sliced
(about 6 ounces)

4 teaspoons pumpkin seeds
2 tablespoons olive oil
2 tablespoons lemon juice
1 tablespoon fresh salad herbs
Large pinch of each curry
and ginger
4 ounces reduced fat goat cheese,
sliced
Salt and pepper to taste

cooking instructions

In a bowl mix the oil, lemon, and herbs. Blend in the curry, ginger, and season to taste.

In a bowl mix the greens with 2/3 of the prepared dressing. Equally divide the greens among four plates. Top with the chicken, fruit, avocado, pumpkin seeds, and goat cheese. Drizzle the remaining dressing and serve immediately.

nutritional facts

Per Serving: 385 Cal (48% from Fat, 28% from Protein, 24% from Carb); 27 g Protein; 21 g Tot Fat; 6 g Sat Fat; 11 g Mono Fat; 24 g Carb; 7 g Fiber; 13 g Sugar; 105 mg Calcium; 2 mg Iron; 169 mg Sodium; 62 mg Cholesterol

Belgium Endives with Gorgonzola

serves 4

ingredients

6 Belgium endives
(about 1 pound)
1/4 cup walnuts, chopped
2 ounces Gorgonzola
2 tablespoons walnut oil
1 tablespoon red wine vinegar

1 tablespoon low-fat milk
mixed with a dash of mashed
Gorgonzola
1 tablespoon fresh salad herbs,
chopped
Salt and pepper to taste

cooking instructions

Mix the oil, vinegar, and milk mixture. Add herbs and season to taste.

Slice the endives. Disregard the trunk of each endive. Wash and dry the
endives with a salad spinner. Transfer to a bowl and mix with the dressing.
Add the walnuts and the crumbled remaining Gorgonzola. Toss lightly
and serve immediately.

nutritional facts

Per Serving: 198 Cal (72% from Fat,
15% from Protein, 14% from Carb);
8 g Protein; 17 g Tot Fat; 4 g Sat
Fat; 4 g Mono Fat; 7 g Carb; 6 g
Fiber; 1 g Sugar; 244 mg Calcium;
2 mg Iron; 87 mg Sodium; 16 mg
Cholesterol

Grapefruit and Crabmeat Salad

serves 2

ingredients

1 large pink grapefruit
(about 16 ounces grapefruit)
8 ounces crabmeat portions,
excess water removed
2 tablespoons low-fat canola
mayonnaise

1 cup lettuce, shredded
1 tablespoon freshly minced
cilantro
Chili powder to taste
Salt and pepper to taste

cooking instructions

Place the crabmeat in a bowl.

Cut the grapefruit in half. Insert a thin knife all around the skin to loosen up the flesh. Separate the flesh from the skin and place it on a cutting board. Dice the flesh small and transfer to the crabmeat bowl. Add mayonnaise, chili powder, cilantro, and season to taste. Cover with plastic wrap and refrigerate for half an hour.

Equally divide the lettuce in two plates and top with the prepared grapefruit crabmeat salad.

nutritional facts

Per Serving (4 ounces crabmeat):
219 Cal (19% from Fat, 43% from
Protein, 38% from Carb); 24 g Protein; 5 g Tot Fat; 1 g Sat Fat;
1 g Mono Fat; 21 g Carb; 3 g Fiber;
16 g Sugar; 105 mg Calcium;
1 mg Iron; 1240 mg Sodium;
63 mg Cholesterol

Cod and Potato Quiche with Greens

serves 6

ingredients

2 eggs
1 yolk
1 ½ cup regular milk
1/4 teaspoon salt
1/8 teaspoon pepper
1/8 teaspoon nutmeg
3/4 pound cooked cod fish fillet, shredded

1 medium onion, thinly sliced (about 6 ounces)
3 cups shredded potatoes
3 tablespoons plus 1 teaspoon canola oil
1 large Boston lettuce
1/4 cup vinaigrette

cooking instructions

Preheat the oven to 425°F.

Heat 1 teaspoon of oil in a skillet over low heat. Add the onions and cook until soft, but not browned (about 4 to 5 minutes). In a bowl mix the eggs, yolk, milk, salt, pepper, nutmeg, and set aside.

Mix 3 tablespoons of canola oil with the shredded potatoes. Spread them over a 9-inch pie pan, as you would do with pie dough. Bake for 15 minutes or until the edge starts to turn golden brown. Remove from the oven. Spread the cooked onions and cod fish over the bottom of the prepared potato pie pan. Pour the egg mixture over and bake for 25 to 30 minutes or until the custard sets. Remove from the oven and wait 5 minutes before slicing. Meanwhile mix the lettuce with the vinaigrette. Serve each quiche slice on top of the green portion.

nutritional facts

Per Serving: 293 Cal (45% from Fat, 23% from Protein, 32% from Carb); 17 g Protein; 15 g Tot Fat; 3 g Sat Fat; 8 g Mono Fat; 23 g Carb; 2 g Fiber; 6 g Sugar; 115 mg Calcium; 1 mg Iron; 350 mg Sodium; 145 mg Cholesterol

White Beans and Tuna Salad

serves 6

ingredients

2 cups cooked white beans

8 ounces cooked tuna

2 scallions, chopped

2 tomatoes; peeled, seeded, and diced (about 12 ounces)

1 medium yellow bell pepper; cut in half, seeded, and ribs removed (about 6 ounces)

1 tablespoon freshly minced parsley

1 tablespoon freshly minced tarragon

2 tablespoons lemon juice

4 tablespoons olive oil

Salt and pepper to taste

cooking instructions

Preheat the broiler. Place the bell pepper halves, opening down, on a cookie sheet. Broil until the skin is completely browned. Place in a brown bag, seal, and let stand for 10 minutes. Remove the bell pepper skin and dice.

Place the beans, tuna, scallions, and parsley in a bowl. Mix with half the lemon juice and half the olive oil. Season with pepper and salt. Transfer to an elongated platter. Spread the tomatoes, bell pepper pieces and adjust seasonings. Sprinkle with the remaining lemon juice and olive oil before serving.

nutritional facts

Per Serving: 364 Cal (36% from Fat, 26% from Protein, 38% from Carb); 24 g Protein; 15 g Tot Fat; 2 g Sat Fat; 10 g Mono Fat; 36 g Carb; 8 g Fiber; 2 g Sugar; 132 mg Calcium; 5 mg Iron; 35 mg Sodium; 26 mg Cholesterol

Grilled Cheese Sandwich with Dandelion Salad

serves 2

ingredients

4 slices of wheat bread
4 slices of Cheddar Cheese
2 tablespoons grapeseed oil
4 ounces dandelion (about 2 cups)
1/4 small red onion, diced
1 large tomato, diced
(about 8 ounces)
1 tablespoon freshly minced basil
2 tablespoons vinaigrette

cooking instructions

Mix the vinaigrette with the dandelion, tomato, red onion, and basil. Divide between two plates.

Place two cheese slices between two bread slices. Brush the grapeseed oil on the outsides of the bread slices. Heat a skillet or grill. Add the sandwich and brown on both sides.

nutritional facts

Per Serving: 488 Cal (58% from Fat, 14% from Protein, 28% from Carb); 18 g Protein; 32 g Tot Fat; 17 g Sat Fat; 9 g Mono Fat; 35 g Carb; 5 g Fiber; 8 g Sugar; 480 mg Calcium; 4 mg Iron; 820 mg Sodium; 75 mg Cholesterol

Fish/Seafood Entrées

A healthy diet includes plenty of fish. Why? **Fish are sources of proteins, fats, vitamins, and minerals, as well as many essential amino acids.** In addition, one of the best sources for Omega-3 fatty acids are oily fish like cod, tuna, salmon, sardines, herring, and mackerel—and all are easier to digest than meat.

You may have already heard about the health benefits of Omega-3 fatty acids, which help promote weight loss while still having a positive effect on the metabolizing of muscle proteins. Omega-3 fatty acids also help **reduce inflammation and lower bad cholesterol (LDL).** As for shellfish, keep in mind that the protein levels are usually a little lower than fish and, from a nutrition standpoint, can result in higher cholesterol. So be careful not to over-indulge in shellfish.

Cooking fish and shellfish requires particular attention, as the flesh tends to be rather delicate. It is recommended that you use cooking techniques such as steaming, baking, broiling, barbecuing, or sautéing in a nonstick pan with very little oil.

Broiled Salmon with Orange Salsa

serves 4

ingredients

1 1/2 tablespoons grapeseed oil
Four 5-ounce salmon fillets
2 mangos, diced
(about 14 ounces)
1 orange, diced (about 6 ounces)
1 small red onion, diced
(about 2 ounces)

2 green jalapenos, diced
1 bunch of cilantro, chopped
1/4 cup of orange juice
Salt and pepper to taste

cooking instructions

Mix the mangos, orange, red onion, jalapenos, cilantro and orange juice in a bowl. Season to taste and refrigerate at least 30 minutes before use.

Preheat the broiler. Brush oil over the fillets and season lightly. Broil the fish for 5 minutes on the non-skin side first. Turnover, brush more oil, and continue to cook for 5 minutes or until the flesh starts to flake. Serve immediately with the salsa.

nutritional facts

Per Serving: 350 Cal (34% from Fat, 36% from Protein, 30% from Carb); 32 g Protein; 13 g Tot Fat; 3 g Sat Fat; 4 g Mono Fat; 27 g Carb; 3 g Fiber; 21 g Sugar; 387 mg Calcium; 1 mg Iron; 110 mg Sodium; 55 mg Cholesterol

Broiled Salmon with Italian Herbs

serves 4

ingredients

2 tablespoons olive oil
Four 5-ounce salmon fillets
Italian herbs
2 lemons
32 asparagus stalks, trimmed
(about 2 pounds of asparagus)
Salt and pepper to taste

cooking instructions

Preheat the broiler and steamer.

Place the fillets on a greased pan. Brush olive oil and squeeze lemon juice from one lemon over the fillets. Sprinkle with the herbs and season lightly. Broil for 5 minutes. Turn over, brush with oil, and continue to broil for 5 minutes or until the salmon flesh starts to flake.

Meanwhile place the asparagus in the steamer basket and cook until desired tenderness.

Transfer the fish to a serving platter and arrange the asparagus around. Serve immediately with lemon wedges.

nutritional facts

Per Serving: 316 Cal (40% from Fat, 43% from Protein, 17% from Carb); 36 g Protein; 15 g Tot Fat; 3 g Sat Fat; 8 g Mono Fat; 15 g Carb; 7 g Fiber; 4 g Sugar; 440 mg Calcium; 6 mg Iron; 113 mg Sodium

Honey Glazed Salmon

serves 4

✔ *Serve with Vegetables Gratin (see page 110).*

ingredients

Four 5-ounce salmon fillets
2 tablespoons Dijon mustard
4 teaspoons honey
2 teaspoons freshly minced thyme
1 lime
Salt and pepper to taste

cooking instructions

Place the salmon fillets in a microwave safe dish.

In a bowl, mix the mustard, honey, thyme, and season to taste. Spread the mixture evenly over the salmon fillets. Sprinkle with a little lime juice and cover with a microwaveable top or loosely with plastic wrap. Microwave on high for 3 to 4 minutes. Time may vary based on the thickness of your fillets. Remove from the microwave and let stand for 2 minutes before serving.

nutritional facts

Per Serving: 296 Cal (48% from Fat, 39% from Protein, 13% from Carb); 29 g Protein; 16 g Tot Fat; 3 g Sat Fat; 6 g Mono Fat; 10 g Carb; 2 g Fiber; 7 g Sugar; 47 mg Calcium; 2 mg Iron; 173 mg Sodium; 84 mg Cholesterol

Baked Sardines with Collard Greens

serves 4

ingredients

Four 5-ounce sardines
2 tablespoons olive oil
1 large onion, sliced
(about 8 ounces)
2 pounds collard greens; washed,
ribs removed, and pat dry
3 garlic cloves, minced

1/3 cup low-fat milk
1/4 cup fresh parsley, minced
1 teaspoon freshly minced thyme
2 pinches nutmeg
4 tablespoons shredded parmesan
1 tablespoon almond meal
Salt and pepper to taste

cooking instructions

Preheat the oven to 375°F.

Remove the heads from sardines and clean their insides well (this can be done at the fish market). Rinse well under cold water.

Blanch the collard greens in salted water until barely tender. Drain and press to remove excess water. Chop the collard greens.

Heat 1 tablespoon olive oil in a nonstick pan over medium heat. Add the onion and sauté until translucent. Add the garlic, collard greens, and cook for 2 minutes mixing constantly. Sprinkle and mix in the almond meal. Add the milk, 2 tablespoons parmesan, parsley, thyme, nutmeg, and season to taste.

Pour the mixture on to a greased baking dish and slide in the sardines. Sprinkle the remaining parmesan and drizzle 1 tablespoon olive oil. Cover and bake for 20 to 25 minutes.

nutritional facts

Per Serving: 390 Cal (51% from Fat, 33% from Protein, 16% from Carb); 32 g Protein; 22 g Tot Fat; 5 g Sat Fat; 11 g Mono Fat; 16 g Carb; 5 g Fiber; 4 g Sugar; 365 mg Calcium; 3 mg Iron; 259 mg Sodium; 92 mg Cholesterol

Poached Oysters with Leeks and Kale

serves 4

ingredients

1 tablespoon olive oil
24 oysters
1 shallot, minced
1 garlic clove, minced
2 large leeks (about 1 pound 6 ounces)
3 tablespoons crème fraiche

2 pounds kale
2 lemons
Salad herbs, minced
Pinch Nutmeg
Salt and pepper to taste

cooking instructions

Trim the leeks keeping only the white part. Cut in half, clean, and chop small.

Carefully open the oysters and transfer their water to a bowl. Remove their flesh and set aside. Place the shells in a large bowl. Zest half a lemon.

Blanch the kale in salted water until tender. Press to remove excess water. Chop small and set aside.

Heat a large pan with water and bring to boil. Meanwhile heat the oil in a pan over high heat. Add the shallot, garlic, leek, and sauté until tender. Add the kale, a little lemon juice, lemon zest, nutmeg, oyster water, herbs, and crème fraiche. Stir well and bring to a simmer. Reduce heat and add the oysters. Season to taste and continue to cook another minute. Blanch the oyster shells in the boiling water and transfer to a serving platter. Fill each oyster shell with the prepared mixture and serve immediately with lemon wedges.

nutritional facts

Per Serving: 428 Cal (29% from Fat, 31% from Protein, 40% from Carb); 35 g Protein; 15 g Tot Fat; 4 g Sat Fat; 5 g Mono Fat; 45 g Carb; 8 g Fiber; 5 g Sugar; 279 mg Calcium; 19 mg Iron; 925 mg Sodium; 160 mg Cholesterol

Tuna with Broccoli and Sesame Vinaigrette

serves 4

ingredients

Four 5-ounce tuna fillets
2 1/2 large heads broccoli florets
(about 1 1/2 pounds)
1 teaspoon of Wasabi
1 shallot, minced
2 garlic cloves, minced
1 teaspoon minced ginger
2 tablespoons sesame oil

1 cup canola oil
1/2 cup rice vinegar
2 tablespoons soy sauce
3 tablespoons cilantro, minced
Salt and pepper to taste

cooking instructions

Blend the Wasabi, shallot, garlic, ginger, rice vinegar, oils, and soy sauce in a food processor. Add cilantro and season to taste.

Marinade the tuna in half the vinaigrette and refrigerate for an hour. Refrigerate the remaining vinaigrette.

Pat dry the tuna fillets. Heat a pan with a little canola oil on high heat. Add the fillets and brown. Turn over and continue to cook until desired doneness.

Meanwhile blanch the broccoli for one and a half minutes in salted boiling water. Remove and transfer to a bowl. Mix in the remaining vinaigrette and serve immediately with the tuna fillets.

nutritional facts

Per Serving: 536 Cal (59% from Fat, 29% from Protein, 12% from Carb); 39 g Protein; 36 g Tot Fat; 3 g Sat Fat; 19 g Mono Fat; 17 g Carb; 5 g Fiber; 4 g Sugar; 123 mg Calcium; 3 mg Iron; 568 mg Sodium; 64 mg Cholesterol

Spicy Tuna with Avocado Spread

serves 4

ingredients

2 teaspoons olive oil

Four 5-ounce tuna fillets

1 large red onion, diced
(about 8 ounces)

2 large Roma tomatoes,
peeled, seeded, and diced
(about 8 ounces)

2 medium yellow bell peppers;
seeded, ribs removed, and diced
(about 12 ounces)

1 jalapeno, seeded and diced

1 avocado, puréed

4 tablespoons low-fat yogurt

2 tablespoons cilantro

1/2 lime, juiced

Tabasco

Cajun spices

Salt and pepper to taste

cooking instructions

Mix the avocado with the lime juice. Mix in the yogurt, jalapeno chiles, cilantro, and season to taste. Add Tabasco to taste and refrigerate until needed.

Preheat the broiler. Sprinkle Cajun spices on both sides of the fillets. Place the fillets on a greased baking sheet and broil for 2 to 3 minutes. Turn over and continue to cook for 3 to 4 minutes or until the fish flesh starts to flake. Slightly salt when the fish is done.

Meanwhile heat the remaining oil in a large pan over medium heat. Add the onion and sauté until translucent. Add the yellow bell peppers and continue to sauté for 2 minutes. Mix in the tomatoes and cook for 2 more minutes. Add a little Cajun spices and lightly salt.

Plate the vegetables, top with the tuna, avocado spread, and serve immediately.

nutritional facts

Per Serving: 340 Cal (35% from Fat, 42% from Protein, 23% from Carb); 37 g Protein; 13 g Tot Fat; 2 g Sat Fat; 8 g Mono Fat; 20 g Carb; 6 g Fiber; 6 g Sugar; 80 mg Calcium; 2 mg Iron; 72 mg Sodium; 66 mg Cholesterol

Sole Meunière

serves 4

ingredients

Four 5-ounce sole fillets
4 tablespoons grapeseed oil
2 ounces sliced almonds
1 tablespoon lemon juice
1 tablespoon freshly minced parsley

1 lemon, quartered
24 ounces green beans
1 lemon
Salt and pepper to taste

cooking instructions

Preheat the oven to 400°F. Trim and wash the green beans.

Cover a cookie sheet with parchment paper. Spread the sliced almonds and bake until golden brown. Remove from the oven and set aside.

Place the green beans in a pan and fill with enough water to cover. Add 1 teaspoon of salt. Bring to boil. Reduce heat and simmer until tender. Strain and transfer to a serving plate, sprinkle lemon juice, and season to taste.

Season the sole fillets to taste. Heat 1 tablespoon grapeseed oil in a nonstick pan over medium heat. Add the fillets and cook for 2 to 3 minutes. Carefully turn over and continue to cook 3 minutes or until cooked through.

Place the fillets in a serving platter and sprinkle withthe almonds. Cover to keep warm. Place the remaining oil, lemon juice, and parsley into a pan. Bring to a boil and pour over the sole fillets.

Serve immediately with green beans and lemon wedges.

nutritional facts

Per Serving: 395 Cal (48% from Fat, 32% from Protein, 20% from Carb); 34 g Protein; 23 g Tot Fat; 3 g Sat Fat; 15 g Mono Fat; 21 g Carb; 10 g Fiber; 3 g Sugar; 158 mg Calcium; 3 mg Iron; 128 mg Sodium; 68 mg Cholesterol

Mackerels with Mushrooms

serves 4

ingredients

Four 5-ounce mackerels
4 tomatoes (about 1 1/2 pounds)
2 lemons, cleaned and sliced
8 large white mushrooms, skin
removed and sliced (about 8
ounces)
4 teaspoons Dijon mustard
4 pinches Herbs de Provence
(or Italian herbs)

1 tablespoon garlic cloves,
minced
2 tablespoons freshly minced
parsley
Salt and pepper to taste

For the vegetables:
2 pounds green beans
1 lemon
Salt and pepper to taste

cooking instructions

Preheat the oven to 400°F. Trim and wash the green beans. Set aside.

Season the inside of the mackerels. Prepare four aluminum foils to fit the mackerels. On each foil place 2 lemon slices, 2 tomato slices, a little garlic, and a few mushroom slices. Add one mackerel and spread 1 teaspoon mustard over it. Sprinkle with1 pinch of Herbs de Provence. Top with 2 lemon slices, 2 tomato slices, more mushrooms, and parsley. Close the foil, place in a baking dish, and bake for 20 to 25 minutes.

Place the green beans in a pan and fill with enough water to cover. Add 1 teaspoon salt and bring to boil. Reduce heat and simmer until cooked through. Strain and transfer to a serving bowl. Sprinkle with lemon juice and season to taste. Serve the mackerels, their vegetables and juices, with the green beans.

nutritional facts

Per Serving: 451 Cal (42% from Fat, 30% from Protein, 28% from Carb); 36 g Protein; 22 g Tot Fat; 5 g Sat Fat; 8 g Mono Fat; 34 g Carb; 13 g Fiber; 4 g Sugar; 167 mg Calcium; 6 mg Iron; 422 mg Sodium; 107 mg Cholesterol

Mackerels en Papilotte

serves 4

ingredients

For the fish:
Four 5-ounce mackerels
4 teaspoons minced garlic
4 tablespoons olive oil
4 tablespoons freshly minced
parsley
1 lemon
Salt and pepper to taste

For the vegetables:
2 teaspoons olive oil
1 pound dandelion
1 small onion, sliced
(about 4 ounces)
2 garlic cloves, minced
Salt and pepper to taste

cooking instructions

Preheat the oven to 350°F.

Place each mackerel on a greased aluminum foil and season the inside. Sprinkle with the garlic, oil, parsley, some lemon juice, and season to taste. Close the foils tight and place on a baking dish. Bake for 20 minutes.

Meanwhile place the dandelions in a pan and add a little salted water. Cook for 10 minutes mixing occasionally. Add water, if necessary to avoid burning. Remove and strain.

Heat the oil in a pan over high heat. Add the onion and sauté until translucent. Add the garlic, dandelions, and season to taste. Sauté for 2 minutes and serve immediately with the mackerels.

nutritional facts

Per Serving: 613 Cal (52% from Fat, 21% from Protein, 27% from Carb); 33 g Protein; 37 g Tot Fat; 7 g Sat Fat; 19 g Mono Fat; 43 g Carb; 8 g Fiber; 7 g Sugar; 281 mg Calcium; 7 mg Iron; 224 mg Sodium; 99 mg Cholesterol

Herrings with Potatoes and Onions

serves 4

ingredients

Four 4-ounce herrings
1 teaspoon canola oil
2 teaspoons olive oil
1 large onion, sliced
(about 8 ounces)
4 small red potatoes
(about 3 ounces each)

1 tablespoon garlic cloves,
minced
1 bunch fresh parsley, minced
dash of white vinegar
Salt and pepper to taste

cooking instructions

Preheat the oven to 400° F.

Place the potatoes into a pan and cover with water. Add 1 teaspoon salt and bring to a boil over high heat. Reduce heat and simmer for 15 minutes. When barely cooked, strain and let cool a bit. Peel and slice the potatoes. Heat the canola oil in a nonstick pan over high heat. Add the onions and slightly brown. Add the garlic and continue to cook for 1 minute. Remove from heat and cool. Place each herring on a piece of aluminum foil. Open the herrings and sprinkle with a little pepper. Equally divide the potatoes and onions among the herrings. Sprinkle with olive oil andparsley. Close the foils tight and place in a baking dish. Bake for 25 to 30 minutes. Serve immediately with a dash of white vinegar.

nutritional facts

Per Serving (4 ounces herring):
471 Cal (34% from Fat, 27% from Protein, 39% from Carb); 32 g Protein; 18 g Tot Fat; 4 g Sat Fat; 8 g Mono Fat; 46 g Carb; 8 g Fiber; 4 g Sugar; 141 mg Calcium; 8 mg Iron; 1061 mg Sodium; 93 mg Cholesterol

Shrimp Scampi Style

serves 4

ingredients

4 tablespoons olive oil
12 ounces shrimp
1 large onion, sliced
(about 8 ounces)
2 large yellow bell peppers;
seeded, ribs removed, and sliced
(about 1 pound)
4 large garlic cloves, minced

1 lemon
4 tablespoons freshly minced
basil
8 ounces whole wheat pasta
(about 2 cups)
Salt and pepper to taste

cooking instructions

Cook the pasta according to package directions.

Heat 2 tablespoons of oil and the garlic in a large pan over medium heat. Add the shrimp and cook for a minute stirring occasionally. In another pan, heat the remaining oil. Add the onion and sauté until translucent. Add the bell pepper and sauté for 2 minutes. Add a little lemon juice, basil, shrimp, cooked pasta, and season to taste. Mix, continuing to cook until desired tenderness, and serve immediately.

nutritional facts

Per Serving: 475 Cal (29% from Fat, 22% from Protein, 49% from Carb); 28 g Protein; 16 g Tot Fat; 2 g Sat Fat; 10 g Mono Fat; 61 g Carb; 4 g Fiber; 5 g Sugar; 134 mg Calcium; 5 mg Iron; 138 mg Sodium; 129 mg Cholesterol

Scallops with Orange Sauce

serves 4

ingredients

1 tablespoon olive oil

1 pound scallops

6 tangerines

1 cup orange juice

1 teaspoon minced ginger

1 shallot, minced

8 ounces mushrooms

2 tablespoons parsley, minced

Olive oil

Salt and pepper

cooking instructions

Peel and segment the tangerines. Place the orange juice and half of the ginger in a saucepan and bring to a boil over high heat. Reduce until you end up with 1/4 cup and set aside.

Heat 1 teaspoon of olive oil in a saucepan over high heat. Add the mushrooms, shallot, remaining ginger, and sauté quickly. Add parsley and season to taste.

Meanwhile, lightly season the scallops. Heat 2 teaspoons of olive oil in a large saucepan over high heat. Add the scallops and sear on both sides. Add the mandarin segments, reduced orange juice, and continue to sauté for 1 minute. Serve immediately with the mushrooms and drizzle with a little olive oil.

nutritional facts

Per Serving: 241 Cal (18% from Fat, 36% from Protein, 46% from Carb); 22 g Protein; 5 g Tot Fat; 1 g Sat Fat; 3 g Mono Fat; 29 g Carb; 4 g Fiber; 19 g Sugar; 62 mg Calcium; 1 mg Iron; 189 mg Sodium; 37 mg Cholesterol

Meat/Poultry/Vegetable Entrées

I t is important to your health to make sure you get the right amount of a good lean source of protein. You may already know that **animal protein is not as healthy for you as other, leaner protein sources** such as beans or tofu; this is because meat can raise cholesterol levels. Seek out organic meat and poultry (or free-range). This is healthier for you, due to the animal's natural diet, which results in higher amounts of beneficial fats such as Omega-3.

Here are some good general rules for selecting meat: **choose white meat such as chicken or turkey breast over darker meat.** Favor skinless pieces and, if cooking with the skin, avoid eating poultry cooked skin which is loaded with fat. Note that beef, lamb, mutton, and pork, which are higher in fat, should be eaten sparingly, and this is why this book features only a few recipes with these meats. When you do eat them, choose tender loin cuts. Choose buffalo or venison over beef. Avoid sausages, bacon, and pâtés due to their high unhealthy fat content. **Employ healthy cooking techniques such as baking, broiling, grilling, barbecuing, or sautéing in a nonstick pan with very little oil.** This limits the addition of fat and calories during preparation while preserving the succulent flavor of the meats.

Tofu with Stir-fried Vegetables

serves 4

ingredients

2 teaspoons canola oil
1 medium onion, sliced (about 6 ounces)
2 medium carrots, thinly sliced diagonally (about 6 ounces)
1 medium red bell pepper, sliced (about 6 ounces)
3 large garlic cloves, minced
1 inch of ginger, minced
1 large head of broccoli florets (about 8 ounces)
4 baby Bok Choy, sliced
1/2 cup sugar snap pea pods (about 2 1/2 ounces)

A few pinches Chinese Five Spices
1 cup soy sprouts (about 3 ounces)
2 tablespoons freshly minced parsley
2 tablespoons freshly minced cilantro
1/4 cup soy sauce mixed with 2 teaspoons cornstarch
1 teaspoon sesame oil
1 tablespoon sesame seeds
12 ounces firm tofu, diced
Pepper to taste

cooking instructions

Heat the oil in a large wok or saucepan over high heat. Add the onion and cook until translucent. Add the carrots, garlic, and ginger. Cook until the carrots are tender. Add the broccoli, bell pepper, Boy Choy, sugar snap peas, spices, and cook for 2 minutes. Add tofu, soy sprouts, parsley, cilantro, and cook for 1 minute. Add the soy sauce mixture and mix well while thickening. Add the sesame oil and sesame seeds. Adjust seasoning and serve immediately.

nutritional facts

Per Serving: 263 Cal (31% from Fat, 20% from Protein, 49% from Carb); 14 g Protein; 10 g Tot Fat; 1 g Sat Fat; 4 g Mono Fat; 35 g Carb; 6 g Fiber; 9 g Sugar; 177 mg Calcium; 5 mg Iron; 1303 mg Sodium; 0 mg Cholesterol

Tofu and Collard Greens Burgers

serves 4

ingredients

8 ounces tofu
6 ounces cooked collard greens
1 small onion, diced
(about 4 ounces)
1 small carrot, shredded
(about 2 ounces)
2 scallions, chopped
2 garlic cloves, minced
1 1/3 cup water crackers

4 teaspoons almond butter
2 tablespoons minced salad herbs
Salt and pepper to taste
4 slices of cheddar cheese (about
4 ounces)

cooking instructions

Mix all the ingredients, except cheese, in a food processor until well combined. Form 4 patties and grill on each side for 4 to 5 minutes. Melt the cheese on top and serve immediately.

nutritional facts

Per Serving: 277 Cal (38% from Fat, 21% from Protein, 41% from Carb); 15 g Protein; 12 g Tot Fat; 5 g Sat Fat; 4 g Mono Fat; 29 g Carb; 4 g Fiber; 4 g Sugar; 314 mg Calcium; 3 mg Iron; 345 mg Sodium; 20 mg Cholesterol

Chicken Breasts with Garlic Cloves

serves 4

ingredients

Four 5-ounce skinless chicken breasts
2 teaspoons canola oil
1 ¼ cup garlic cloves, peeled
1 cup chicken stock (low-fat and low-sodium)
1 sprig fresh thyme
1 sprig fresh rosemary
1 laurel leaf
Cornstarch plus water
Salt and pepper to taste

For the vegetables:
1 tablespoon canola oil
3 medium white potatoes, washed, pat dry, and quartered (about 1 pound)

2 medium carrots, chopped (about 6 ounces)
1 large head broccoli florets (about 12 ounces)
1 medium red onion, quartered (about 6 ounces)
1 large red bell pepper, chopped (about 6 ounces)
3 garlic cloves, minced
1 sprig fresh thyme, minced
1 sprig fresh rosemary, minced
1 laurel leaf, minced
1/2 lemon, juiced
Salt, pepper, and paprika

nutritional facts

Per Serving: 497 Cal (20% from Fat, 41% from Protein, 40% from Carb); 50 g Protein; 11 g Tot Fat; 2 g Sat Fat; 5 g Mono Fat; 49 g Carb; 7 g Fiber; 7 g Sugar; 185 mg Calcium; 4 mg Iron; 298 mg Sodium; 109 mg Cholesterol

cooking instructions

Preheat the oven to 425°F.

For the vegetables:
Place the potatoes and carrots in a baking pan. Mix in 2 teaspoons oil and sprinkle with paprika. Bake for 25 minutes. Add the red onions, red bell peppers, broccoli, garlic, minced herbs, a little more oil, sprinkle pepper, and mix well. Continue to bake for 15 to 20 minutes. Sprinkle salt before serving.

> ✓ *Tip: The amount of cornstarch and water mixture may vary depending on the amount of water rendered by the chicken and the reduction process. To obtain the right thickness for a sauce: dip a spoon in the sauce, turn it over, and make a line across with your finger. Tilt over the spoon. If the sauce does not run over the line, it is the perfect thickness. If it does, you need to thicken with a little cornstarch water mixture. After adding this, you will need to bring the sauce to a boil. Also, if it gets too thick, just add a little liquid to thin out.*

For the chicken:
Heat the oil in a nonstick pan over high heat. Add the chicken breasts and brown on both sides. Transfer the chicken breasts to a plate.

Deglaze the pan with a little water and add the garlic cloves. Sauté until the cloves are slightly brown. Add the chicken, half cup of stock, lemon juice, 1 thyme branch, 1 rosemary branch, 1 laurel leaf, and bring to boil. Reduce heat, cover, and cook for 15 to 20 minutes or until the chicken is cooked through. Place the chicken breasts and garlic cloves on a serving platter. Cover with aluminum foil to keep warm.

Add the remaining stock and boil until reduced to 3/4 cup. Strain and return to the pan. Thicken with a little cornstarch water mixture. Add any rendered chicken juices, bring to a boil, and adjust seasonings. Pour over the chicken breasts. Serve the chicken with the baked vegetables.

Stuffed Chicken Breast with Boursin

✓ *For a tip on adjusting thickness of the sauce, see page 95.*

serves 4

ingredients

1 tablespoon olive oil
Four 4-ounce chicken breasts
8 fresh large basil leaves
2 ounces Boursin (garlic and herbs), divided into four portions
1 large shallot, thinly sliced
1 cup chicken stock (low-fat and low-sodium)

4 pinches dry Italian herbs
2 tablespoons freshly minced parsley
Cornstarch plus a little water
2 pounds fresh dandelions, washed and pat-dry
Salt and pepper to taste
Twine or toothpick

cooking instructions

Preheat the oven to 350°F.

Place the chicken breasts between two plastic wrap sheets. Flatten with a mallet until fairly thin. Sprinkle pepper and a pinch of Italian herbs on each breast. Spread one portion of Boursin, 2 basil leaves, and roll tightly each breast. Secure with twine or toothpick so it does not unroll on its own.

Heat the oil in a sauté pan over high heat. Add the turkey rolls, placing the folded side face down first. Brown and turn over. Once browned, add the shallot, and half of the chicken stock. Bring to a boil and place in the oven for 10 to 12 minutes. Transfer the rolls to a serving platter and cover with aluminum foil to keep warm. Add the remaining stock and reduce the sauce to less than 1 cup. Thicken with a little cornstarch water mixture. Add the parsley, any rendered turkey juices, and bring to a boil. Adjust seasonings and pour over the turkey. Serve immediately with the steamed dandelions.

While the sauce is reducing, stir-fry the dandelions until slightly wilted. Season to taste and serve with the stuffed chicken.

nutritional facts

Per Serving: 324 Cal (27% from Fat, 43% from Protein, 30% from Carb); 35 g Protein; 10 g Tot Fat; 3 g Sat Fat; 4 g Mono Fat; 25 g Carb; 8 g Fiber; 9 g Sugar; 460 mg Calcium; 8 mg Iron; 324 mg Sodium; 77 mg Cholesterol

Chicken Curry

serves 4

ingredients

2 tablespoons grapeseed oil

2 tablespoons whole wheat flour

2 cups chicken stock
(low-fat and low-sodium)

1 small onion, diced
(about 4 ounces)

1 medium carrot, diced
(about 3 ounces)

2 cups cooked chicken
(skinless breast) diced

1 tablespoon curry powder or to taste

2 Granny Smith apples, peeled
and diced (about 8 ounces)

4 tablespoons raisins, soaked in
water for 1 hour

2 tablespoons parsley, minced

4 tablespoons low-fat Greek
yogurt

1/2 cup brown rice

4 tablespoons ground almonds

Salt and pepper to taste

cooking instructions

Cook the rice according to package instructions.

Heat the oil in a pan over medium heat. Add the onion, carrot, and sauté quickly. Mix in the flour. Add slowly the stock while constantly mixing. Add the curry powder and bring to a boil. Reduce heat and continue to cook until thickened to a sauce consistency stirring often to avoid scorching on the bottom and sides. Add the chicken, apples, raisins, and parsley. Bring to a simmer and continue to cook for 5 minutes. Remove from heat and mix in the yogurt. Adjust seasonings and serve immediately. Once served, sprinkle one tablespoon of almond meal per serving.

nutritional facts

Per Serving: 480 Cal (31% from Fat, 27% from Protein, 42% from Carb); 33 g Protein; 17 g Tot Fat; 3 g Sat Fat; 5 g Mono Fat; 51 g Carb; 5 g Fiber; 17 g Sugar; 101 mg Calcium; 3 mg Iron; 514 mg Sodium; 122 mg Cholesterol

Cornish Hen with Red Cabbage

serves 4

ingredients

2 tablespoons grapeseed oil

2 Cornish hens

4 slices turkey bacon

1 large onion, sliced
(about 8 ounces)

2 Granny Smith apple, sliced
(about 8 ounces)

1 red cabbage, sliced
(about 1 ½ pounds)

4 cups chicken stock (low-fat and
low-sodium)

2 cloves

1 laurel leaf

1 teaspoon caraway seeds

Mustard

Salt and pepper to taste

cooking instructions

Blanch the red cabbage into boiling salted water. Rinse the Cornish hen under cold water, pat dry, and lightly season.

Heat half of the oil in a sauté pan. Sear the Cornish hen on all sides (about 10 minutes).

Heat the remaining oil in a Dutch oven or brasier. Add the bacon, onion, apples, and sweat for two minutes. Add the red cabbage, stock, cloves, laurel leaf, caraway seeds, and bring to boil. Top with the Cornish hen, cover, and cook for 40 to 50 minutes in the oven. Serve with mustard on the side.

nutritional facts

Per Serving: 554 Cal (55% from Fat, 27% from Protein, 18% from Carb); 38 g Protein; 35 g Tot Fat; 8 g Sat Fat; 13 g Mono Fat; 25 g Carb; 6 g Fiber; 15 g Sugar; 138 mg Calcium; 3 mg Iron; 359 mg Sodium; 182 mg Cholesterol

Turkey Breast with Sage Aromas

✓ *Use the turkey meat to make soup, salad, sandwich, etc.*

serves 4

ingredients

2 tablespoons olive oil
1 turkey breast (about 2 pounds)
1 tablespoon ground sage
3 to 4 fresh sage leaves
1/2 cup chicken stock
(low-fat and low-sodium)
Cornstarch
Salt and pepper to taste

cooking instructions

Preheat the oven to 350°F.

Mix the ground sage with a little pepper and spread all over the turkey breast under its skin. Be careful not to break the skin. Brush olive oil over the skin. Place the turkey skin-side up in a roasting pan. Pour the chicken stock in the pan, add the sage leaves, and bake for an hour or until a meat thermometer registers 180°F.

Remove the turkey breast from the pan, cover with aluminum foil to keep warm. Remove the sage leaves from the sauce and thicken with a little cornstarch and water mixture. Adjust seasonings and serve over the turkey breast slices.

nutritional facts

Per Serving: 341 Cal (50% from Fat, 48% from Protein, 2% from Carb); 40 g Protein; 18 g Tot Fat; 4 g Sat Fat; 9 g Mono Fat; 1 g Carb; 0 g Fiber; 0 g Sugar; 32 mg Calcium; 2 mg Iron; 189 mg Sodium; 118 mg Cholesterol

99

Turkey with Cherries

serves 4

ingredients

1 tablespoon grapeseed oil
Four 4-ounce turkey breasts
1 large shallot, minced
1 teaspoon black peppercorns, cracked
2 pinches dry thyme
1 bay leaf
1 cinnamon stick
1 cup pomegranate juice

1 cup brown sauce
1 cup pitted cherries
2 tablespoons crème fraiche
2 tablespoons parsley, minced
1/2 cup brown rice
Salt and pepper to taste

cooking instructions

Preheat the oven to 350°F.

Cook the rice according to the package instructions.

Heat the oil in an ovenproof skillet over high heat. Add the turkey and brown on both sides. Transfer to the oven and continue to cook for 10 minutes. Remove the pan from the oven with oven mitt and transfer the turkey breasts to a plate. Cover to keep warm. Handling the pan with the oven mitt, disregard any fat from the pan. Add the shallots, peppercorns, thyme, bay leaf, cinnamon, pomegranate juice, and deglaze the bottom and sides of the pan. Bring to a boil and reduce by half. Remove cinnamon stick. Add the brown sauce and reduce to 1 cup. Add the cherries and bring to a boil. Add the turkey breasts, any rendered juices, and bring to a boil. Add the crème fraiche and parsley. Bring to a simmer, adjust seasonings, and serve immediately.

nutritional facts

Per Serving: 402 Cal (37% from Fat, 29% from Protein, 35% from Carb); 28 g Protein; 16 g Tot Fat; 4 g Sat Fat; 4 g Mono Fat; 35 g Carb; 1 g Fiber; 11 g Sugar; 41 mg Calcium; 2 mg Iron; 324 mg Sodium; 80 mg Cholesterol

Pork Loins with Prunes

serves 4

ingredients

1 tablespoon grapeseed oil
Four 5-ounce pork loins,
seasoned lightly with pepper
1 medium onion, quartered
(about 6 ounces)
1 large carrot, quartered
(about 4 ounces)
1/2 cup seedless white grapes
1 ½ pounds prunes, pitted

1/2 cup white grape juice,
unsweetened
1 cup beef stock
(low-fat and low-sodium)
1 bay leaf
1/2 teaspoon thyme
Salt and pepper to taste

cooking instructions

Heat 2 teaspoons oil in a saucepan over high heat. Add the onion and slightly brown. Add the carrot and sauté for 2 minutes. Add the prunes, grapes, grape juice, beef stock, and bring to a boil. Reduce heat, cover, and simmer for 20 to 25 minutes. Adjust seasoning.

Heat one teaspoon of oil in a saucepan over high heat. Add the fillets and brown on both sides. Reduce heat and continue to cook for 3 to 4 minutes or until cooked through. Deglaze the pan with a little bit of the prune juices and adjust seasoning. Serve immediately with the remaining prunes mixture.

nutritional facts

Per Serving: 422 Cal (18% from Fat, 31% from Protein, 51% from Carb); 34 g Protein; 9 g Tot Fat; 2 g Sat Fat; 3 g Mono Fat; 56 g Carb; 7 g Fiber; 34 g Sugar; 67 mg Calcium; 3 mg Iron; 263 mg Sodium; 92 mg Cholesterol

Pork Chops with Sauerkraut

serves 4

ingredients

2 teaspoons canola oil
Four 5-ounce pork loins
2 medium red potatoes, peeled
and quartered (about 8 ounces)
2 medium leeks, quartered
(about 8 ounces)
1 large turnip, peeled and
quartered (about 8 ounces)

2 large carrots, peeled and quartered (about 8 ounces)
1 small white cabbage, quartered
(about 8 ounces)
1 garlic clove, cut in half
1 tablespoon salad herbs
Mustard
Salt and pepper to taste

cooking instructions

Preheat a steamer. Add the potatoes and cook for 5 minutes. Add the remaining vegetables and steam until cooked through.

Rub the loins with the garlic clove and season with pepper. Heat the oil in a saucepan over high heat. Add the loins and brown on both sides. Reduce heat, add the herbs, and continue to cook until almost well-done. Time may vary based on the thickness of the loins. Season with salt and serve immediately with the vegetables and mustard on the side.

nutritional facts

Per Serving: 462 Cal (17% from Fat, 36% from Protein, 48% from Carb); 42 g Protein; 9 g Tot Fat; 2 g Sat Fat; 4 g Mono Fat; 55 g Carb; 11 g Fiber; 10 g Sugar; 142 mg Calcium; 8 mg Iron; 166 mg Sodium; 111 mg Cholesterol

Venison with Spicy Raspberry Sauce

serves 4

✓ *Serve with Green Beans and Mushrooms (see page 108).*

ingredients

4 teaspoons grapeseed oil
Four 4-ounce venison steaks
1 large shallot, minced
1/2 teaspoon black peppercorns, crushed (based on how spicy you like)
2 pinches dry thyme
4 tablespoons aged balsamic vinegar
1 cup Cabernet Sauvignon

1 cup raspberries
4 tablespoons demi-glaze (if not available, substitute 8 tablespoons of brown sauce and reduce by half)
2 tablespoons freshly minced parsley
Salt and pepper to taste

cooking instructions

Puree half the raspberries in a food processor. Pass through a sieve and set aside.

Heat the oil in a nonstick pan over medium-high heat. Add the venison steaks and sauté until golden brown. Turn over and continue to cook for 2 to 3 minutes. Transfer the steaks to a plate and cover with aluminum foil to keep warm. Add the shallots, peppercorns, thyme, vinegar, wine, raspberry sauce, and deglaze the pan. Bring to a boil and reduce liquid by half. Add demi-glace, steaks juices, season to taste, and bring to a boil. Add the steaks, remaining raspberries, and continue to simmer for another minute. Serve immediately.

nutritional facts

Per Serving: 250 Cal (32% from Fat, 52% from Protein, 16% from Carb); 27 g Protein; 8 g Tot Fat; 2 g Sat Fat; 2 g Mono Fat; 8 g Carb; 2 g Fiber; 2 g Sugar; 29 mg Calcium; 5 mg Iron; 113 mg Sodium; 96 mg Cholesterol

Lamb Chops with Garlic Spread

serves 4

ingredients

2 tablespoons olive oil

Four 4-ounce loin lamb chops

2 tablespoons minced garlic

2 teaspoons freshly minced parsley

2 teaspoons freshly minced rosemary

1/2 teaspoon dry crushed red pepper

4 cups green beans (about 2 pounds)

Salt and pepper to taste

cooking instructions

Place the green beans in a pan and cover with enough water. Add 1 teaspoon of salt and bring to a boil. Reduce heat and simmer until tender. Drain and transfer to a serving bowl. Add 2 teaspoons olive oil, season to taste, and mix well.

In a bowl; mix 2 teaspoons olive oil, garlic, parsley, rosemary, and dry crushed red pepper. Rub the spread over the lamb chops.

Heat the remaining olive oil in a nonstick pan over medium heat. Add the lamb chops and cook for 3 to 4 minutes on each side or until desired doneness. Serve immediately with the prepared green beans.

nutritional facts

Per Serving: 250 Cal (45% from Fat, 40% from Protein, 15% from Carb); 25 g Protein; 12 g Tot Fat; 3 g Sat Fat; 7 g Mono Fat; 9 g Carb; 4 g Fiber; 2 g Sugar; 60 mg Calcium; 4 mg Iron; 81 mg Sodium; 73 mg Cholesterol (4 ounces lamb chops)

Side Dishes & Snacks

Oftentimes, proteins are the focus of meals. However, you must not forget about the importance of side dishes and snacks. For one thing, their nutritional value can help complete a day's minimum requirements for fiber, vitamin and mineral intake. Once more, **carefully chosen snacks and side dishes keep us from becoming bored with food.** This is key, for it is often boredom that leads us to binge on poor food choices.

Side dishes should emphasize plenty of vegetables and include an appropriate amount of complex carbohydrates based on your daily activities. Emphasize whole grains rather than refined grains, as they contain antioxidants, lignans, and minerals which fight cancer and reduce oxidation in the body.

Always keep the fat content low in your snacks and side dishes. Snacks should also feature fresh food sources such as fruits, and vegetables high in calcium. Nuts are good too, as long as you are not allergic. Low-fat dairies (cottage cheese and yogurt) should also be a priority on your snacks list because they contain calcium, essential vitamins, and live bacterial cultures, which may help you live longer and may fortify your immune system. Purchase plain organic products with live cultures and no sugar added. Add fresh cut fruits, preserves, or honey to provide sweetness.

Asparagus au Gratin

serves 4

ingredients

1 1/2 pounds asparagus (about 24
asparagus)
2 ounces shredded parmesan
cheese (about 3/4 cup)
1/4 cup Italian breadcrumbs
2 tablespoons grapeseed oil
1/2 teaspoon dry mustard
1 tablespoon dry parsley
Salt and pepper to taste

cooking instructions

Preheat the oven to 400°F and a steamer.

Trim the asparagus and add them to the steamer basket.
Cook for 2 minutes covered. Transfer the asparagus to a
greased baking sheet. In a bowl, mix together the cheese,
breadcrumbs, oil, mustard, parsley, and season to taste.
Spread over the asparagus and bake for 10 minutes or until
the mixture is golden brown.

nutritional facts

Per Serving: 183 Cal (54% from Fat,
21% from Protein, 25% from Carb);
10 g Protein; 11 g Tot Fat; 3 g Sat
Fat; 2 g Mono Fat; 12 g Carb; 4 g
Fiber; 4 g Sugar; 212 mg Calcium;
4 mg Iron; 270 mg Sodium; 12 mg
Cholesterol

Broccoli with Parmesan

serves 4

ingredients

1 tablespoon olive oil
2 1/2 large head of broccoli florets
(about 1 1/4 pounds)
1/3 cup grated parmesan cheese
Salt and pepper to taste

cooking instructions

Preheat a steamer. Add the broccoli to the steamer basket, cover, and steam for 2 minutes. Transfer the broccoli to a serving platter. Season to taste and drizzle with olive oil. Spread the cheese and serve immediately.

nutritional facts

Per Serving: 105 Cal (48% from Fat, 25% from Protein, 27% from Carb); 7 g Protein; 6 g Tot Fat; 2 g Sat Fat; 3 g Mono Fat; 8 g Carb; 0 g Fiber; 0 g Sugar; 160 mg Calcium; 1 mg Iron; 166 mg Sodium; 7 mg Cholesterol

Green Beans with Mushrooms

serves 4

ingredients

1 1/2 tablespoons olive oil
1 small onion, sliced
(about 4 ounces)
1 pound green beans, ends
trimmed
1/2 cup mushrooms, sliced
2 garlic cloves, minced

2 pinches fresh thyme, minced
2 tablespoons freshly minced
basil
1 tablespoon freshly minced
parsley
Salt and pepper to taste

cooking instructions

Place the greens beans in a large pan and cover with water. Add 1 teaspoon of salt and bring to a boil over high heat. Reduce heat and simmer until tender. Drain and set aside.

Heat 1 tablespoon of oil in a nonstick pan over medium heat. Add the onion and sauté until translucent. Add the garlic, mushrooms, herbs, and sauté for 2 minutes. Blend in the green beans and remaining oil. Season to taste and serve immediately.

nutritional facts

Per Serving: 94 Cal (46% from Fat,
10% from Protein, 44% from Carb);
3 g Protein; 5 g Tot Fat; 1 g Sat Fat;
4 g Mono Fat; 11 g Carb; 4 g Fiber;
3 g Sugar; 52 mg Calcium;
1 mg Iron; 9 mg Sodium;
0 mg Cholesterol

Pasta with Sun-Dried Tomatoes

serves 4

ingredients

8 ounces wheat Penne
4 teaspoons olive oil
1/2 small onion, diced (about 2 ounces)
1 medium yellow bell peppers, diced (about 6 ounces)
1 medium head of broccoli florets (about 8 ounces)
2 garlic cloves, minced
10 sun-dried tomatoes packed in oil, julienned

1/4 teaspoon red pepper flakes
2 tablespoons pine nuts
A bunch of fresh basil leaves, julienned
1/4 cup grated parmesan cheese
Salt and pepper to taste

cooking instructions

Bring a pan of slightly salted water plus 1 teaspoon of olive oil to a boil. Add the Penne and cook until al dente, about 10 to 12 minutes. Drain and return to the pan. Mix in 1 teaspoon of olive oil.

Heat 2 teaspoons of olive oil in a pan over high heat. Add the onions and sauté until translucent. Add the bell peppers, garlic, and cook for 2 minutes, mixing occasionally. Add the broccoli, sun-dried tomatoes, red pepper flakes, and continue to cook until the vegetables are tender. Add a little bit of the sun-dried tomatoes oil, the pine nuts, basil, and season to taste. Blend in the cooked pasta and serve immediately.

nutritional facts

Per Serving: 347 Cal (29% from Fat, 11% from Protein, 60% from Carb); 10 g Protein; 12 g Tot Fat; 2 g Sat Fat; 6 g Mono Fat; 55 g Carb; 7 g Fiber; 1 g Sugar; 111 mg Calcium; 2 mg Iron; 134 mg Sodium; 6 mg Cholesterol

Vegetables Gratin

serves 4

ingredients

1 large yellow squash, chopped large (about 8 ounces)

1 large red bell pepper; seeded, ribs removed, and chopped large (about 8 ounces)

1 medium head of broccoli florets (about 6 ounces)

1 large zucchini, chopped large (about 8 ounces)

1 large onion, quartered (about 8 ounces)

2 medium sweet potatoes, chopped large (about 8 ounces)

2 garlic cloves, minced

2 tablespoons lemon juice

2 tablespoons olive oil

1 fresh thyme branches, minced

2 tablespoons freshly minced parsley

2 tablespoons grated parmesan cheese

Salt and pepper to taste

cooking instructions

Cut the vegetables the same size for even cooking.

In a bowl mix the garlic, lemon juice, thyme, parsley, and season to taste. Mix in the remaining vegetables (except sweet potatoes) and set aside for at least an hour.

Preheat the oven to 425°F. Place the sweet potatoes in a roasting pan. Mix in half of the olive oil, sprinkle with pepper, and bake for 20 minutes. Sprinkle the remaining oil over the potatoes. Add the prepared vegetables with the marinade and continue to bake for 20 minutes. Sprinkle the cheese, brown under the broiler, and serve immediately.

nutritional facts

Per Serving: 197 Cal (40% from Fat, 13% from Protein, 47% from Carb); 7 g Protein; 9 g Tot Fat; 2 g Sat Fat; 6 g Mono Fat; 25 g Carb; 4 g Fiber; 9 g Sugar; 147 mg Calcium; 2 mg Iron; 145 mg Sodium; 6 mg Cholesterol

Rice with Lentils

serves 4

ingredients

2/3 cup brown rice
1 1/4 cup lentils, rinsed
(about 5 ounces)
1 large onion, diced (about 8
ounces)
2 garlic cloves, minced
1 teaspoon olive oil
1/2 teaspoon ground cumin

1/2 teaspoon ground coriander
1/2 teaspoon paprika
2 tablespoons freshly minced
parsley
Salt and pepper to taste

cooking instructions

Place the lentils in a pan and cover with water. Bring to a boil over high heat and simmer for 10 minutes. Strain and set aside.

Heat the oil in a large pan over high heat. Add the onions and sauté until translucent. Add the garlic, lentils, seasonings, and 6 cups of water. Bring to a boil. Cover, reduce heat, and simmer for 10 minutes. Add the rice, cover again, and cook for 20 minutes or until tender. Adjust seasonings and remove from heat. Set aside covered for 5 minutes before serving.

nutritional facts

Per Serving: 184 Cal (11% from Fat, 13% from Protein, 76% from Carb); 6 g Protein; 2 g Tot Fat; 0 g Sat Fat; 1 g Mono Fat; 36 g Carb; 5 g Fiber; 3 g Sugar; 36 mg Calcium; 2 mg Iron; 7 mg Sodium; 0 mg Cholesterol

Potato Parsnip Purée

serves 4

ingredients

4 medium white potatoes
(about 1 1/2 pounds)
2 large garlic cloves, peeled
1 small parsnip (about 3 ounces)
1/4 cup low-fat milk
1/2 tablespoon fresh parsley,
minced

1/2 tablespoon fresh chives,
minced
2 teaspoons olive oil
Salt and pepper to taste

cooking instructions

Peel and quarter the potatoes and parsnip. Place them in a deep
pan and add enough cold water to cover them. Add the garlic
cloves, 1/4 teaspoon salt, and bring to a boil over high heat.
Cook until tender, about 20 to 25 minutes. Pass through a sieve,
keeping some of the cooking liquid, and purée with a potato
masher. Add low-fat milk, olive oil, and mix quickly. If too thick,
add a little cooking liquid to get to the right consistency. Mix in
the parsley, chives, and season to taste. Serve immediately.

nutritional facts

Per Serving: 158 Cal (12% from Fat,
9% from Protein, 79% from Carb);
4 g Protein; 2 g Tot Fat; 0 g Sat Fat;
1 g Mono Fat; 32 g Carb; 5 g Fiber;
4 g Sugar; 44 mg Calcium;
1 mg Iron; 20 mg Sodium;
1 mg Cholesterol

Potatoes Au Gratin

serves 4

ingredients

4 large potatoes, thinly sliced
(about 2 pounds)
1 cup low-fat milk
2 garlic cloves, minced
1/2 teaspoon salt
1/8 teaspoon pepper
4 tablespoons grated parmesan
cheese

cooking instructions

Preheat the oven to 425°F.

Place the potato slices overlapping each other in an oven dish
just big enough for them to fit in. Heat the milk, garlic, salt, and
pepper in a pan over medium heat. Bring to a boil and pour over
the potatoes. Place the dish in the oven and bake for 20 minutes.
Sprinkle the cheese and continue to cook for 10 minutes or until
the potatoes are tender. If the cheese is not browned enough, just
place under the broiler for 1 or 2 minutes. If the cheese starts to
burn, cover with aluminum foil.

nutritional facts

Per Serving: 265 Cal (11% from Fat,
13% from Protein, 76% from Carb);
9 g Protein; 3 g Tot Fat; 2 g Sat
Fat; 1 g Mono Fat; 51 g Carb; 4 g
Fiber; 5 g Sugar; 165 mg Calcium;
1 mg Iron; 426 mg Sodium; 10 mg
Cholesterol

Roasted Pumpkin

serves 4

> ✓ You can also use the cooked pumpkin to make a purée or soup. Thin out with low-fat milk until the necessary consistency is reached. You can also use the cooked pumpkin as a base for dips or as a dessert base.

ingredients

3 pounds sugar pumpkin
1 tablespoon grapeseed oil
Salt and pepper to taste
Pumpkin pie spices mix

cooking instructions

Cut open the pumpkin, remove seeds and clean the inside with a spoon. Brush oil inside the cavity, season to taste, and place opening side down on a baking sheet. Roast for 30 to 45 minutes or until tender. Cut out and sprinkle with a little pumpkin pie spices before serving.

nutritional facts

Per Serving: 146 Cal (24% from Fat, 9% from Protein, 67% from Carb); 4 g Protein; 4 g Tot Fat; 1 g Sat Fat; 1 g Mono Fat; 28 g Carb; 10 g Fiber; 11 g Sugar; 88 mg Calcium; 5 mg Iron; 17 mg Sodium; 0 mg Cholesterol

Macaroni and Cheese

serves 6

✓ *Gruyère cheese is what makes this dish so unique. However if not available, you may substitute Swiss cheese.*

ingredients

8 ounces whole wheat macaroni
2 tablespoons grapeseed oil
4 ounces Gruyère cheese, finely
shredded
1/4 cup low-fat milk, hot
Pinch of nutmeg, mixed
with the milk
Salt and pepper to taste

cooking instructions

Cook the pasta according to the package directions.
Strain and return the pasta to the pan.

Mix in the oil with the pasta. Add the Gruyère and
flavored milk. Heat on low heat, mixing constantly and
cook until the cheese is melted. Remove from heat,
season to taste, and serve immediately.

nutritional facts

Per Serving: 170 Cal (55% from Fat,
18% from Protein, 27% from Carb);
8 g Protein; 10 g Tot Fat; 6 g Sat
Fat; 3 g Mono Fat; 11 g Carb;
0 g Fiber; 1 g Sugar; 207 mg Calcium; 0 mg Iron; 69 mg Sodium;
32 mg Cholesterol

Mushrooms and Parmesan Polenta

serves 4

ingredients

3 tablespoons olive oil
3 cups water
1 cup polenta
1/4 teaspoon salt
1/4 cup Parmesan
1/4 small onion, diced
(about 1 ounce)

4 large mushrooms, thinly sliced
(about 4 ounces)
1 tablespoon minced garlic
1 tablespoon freshly minced
parsley
Pepper to taste

cooking instructions

Bring salted water to a boil in a pan over high heat. Gradually add the polenta. Reduce heat and simmer, stirring frequently to prevent scorching, until the mixture thickens. Stir in 2 tablespoons of olive oil. Transfer to a greased bowl and let the polenta set for 10 minutes.

Heat 1 tablespoon of oil in a pan over high heat. Add the onion and sauté until translucent. Add the garlic, mushrooms, and sauté for 2 to 3 minutes. Add the parsley and season to taste.

Invert the polenta on a plate and slice. Transfer the slices to a serving platter, top with the mushroom mixture, shredded cheese, and serve immediately.

nutritional facts

Per Serving: 285 Cal (45% from Fat, 12% from Protein, 42% from Carb); 9 g Protein; 14 g Tot Fat; 4 g Sat Fat; 9 g Mono Fat; 30 g Carb; 3 g Fiber; 1 g Sugar; 153 mg Calcium; 2 mg Iron; 212 mg Sodium; 11 mg Cholesterol

Roasted Potatoes with Artichokes

serves 4

ingredients

8 ounces frozen baby artichokes
4 medium red potatoes, quartered
(about one pound)
2 medium onions, quartered
(about 12 ounces)
2 large tomatoes, quartered
(about 12 ounces)

2 garlic cloves, minced
1 tablespoon lemon juice
3 tablespoons olive oil
1 teaspoon freshly minced
rosemary
Salt and pepper to taste

cooking instructions

Preheat the oven to 425°F.

Cook the artichokes according to package directions and set aside.

Heat 2 tablespoons of olive oil in a pan over high heat. Add the garlic, rosemary, and lemon juice. Sauté briefly and remove from heat. Let stand for 5 minutes and strain. Place the potatoes and onions in a baking dish and mix in the flavored oil. Season to taste and bake for 35 minutes. Remove from the oven, add the artichokes, tomatoes, adjust seasoning, and continue to cook for 10 minutes. Drizzle with a little hot olive oil before serving.

nutritional facts

Per Serving: 315 Cal (29% from Fat, 8% from Protein, 63% from Carb); 7 g Protein; 11 g Tot Fat; 1 g Sat Fat; 8 g Mono Fat; 52 g Carb; 8 g Fiber; 6 g Sugar; 68 mg Calcium; 2 mg Iron; 68 mg Sodium; 0 mg Cholesterol

Broiled Cauliflower

serves 1

ingredients

4 cups cauliflower florets
(about one pound)
1 tablespoon grapeseed oil
1/4 cup breadcrumbs
1/4 cup shredded Swiss cheese
1 tablespoon Italian herbs
Salt and pepper to taste

cooking instructions

Preheat the broiler and a steamer.

Place cauliflower in a steam basket and cook for 5 minutes or until desired doneness. Transfer the florets to a baking dish just large enough to fit the florets tightly. Mix the breadcrumbs, cheese, and herbs in a bowl. Season to taste and sprinkle the mixture over the prepared florets. Broil until golden brown and serve immediately.

nutritional facts

Per Serving: 115 Cal (46% from Fat,
17% from Protein, 37% from Carb);
5 g Protein; 6 g Tot Fat; 2 g Sat Fat;
1 g Mono Fat; 11 g Carb; 3 g Fiber;
3 g Sugar; 114 mg Calcium;
2 mg Iron; 96 mg Sodium;
8 mg Cholesterol

Dandelion with Garlic

serves 4

ingredients

2 pounds fresh dandelion greens
2 tablespoons olive oil
2 garlic cloves, minced
1/4 cup vegetable or chicken
stock (low-fat and low-sodium)
Salt and pepper to taste

cooking instructions

Thoroughly clean the dandelion and dry. Cut the dandelion in half.

Heat the oil and garlic in a saucepan over medium heat. Add the dandelion and cook for 5 minutes. Add the stock and season to taste. Continue to cook for another 5 minutes or until tender. Serve immediately.

nutritional facts

Per Serving: 177 Cal (38% from Fat, 14% from Protein, 48% from Carb); 7 g Protein; 8 g Tot Fat; 1 g Sat Fat; 5 g Mono Fat; 24 g Carb; 8 g Fiber; 9 g Sugar; 438 mg Calcium; 7 mg Iron; 224 mg Sodium; 0 mg Cholesterol

Butternut Squash with Cinnamon

serves 4

ingredients

2 pounds butternut squash
1 orange (about 6 ounces)
3 tablespoons maple syrup
1 teaspoon cinnamon
1 1/2 tablespoons grapeseed oil
Salt and pepper to taste

cooking instructions

Preheat the oven to 350°F.

Remove two large zest strips from the orange. Mince and set aside. Juice the orange and set aside.

Halve the squash lengthwise and remove the seeds and strings. Rub the inside with grapeseed oil and season to taste. Place on a greased cookie sheet, skin side down, and bake for 35 to 40 minutes or until tender.

Meanwhile heat the orange juice, maple syrup, and cinnamon in a pan over high heat. Reduce by half.

Remove the squash from the oven, scoop out the flesh, and transfer to a food processor. Add the orange zest, 1 tablespoon of the concentrated juice, and purée. Add more concentrated juice as needed to reach the desired thickness. Adjust seasonings and serve immediately.

nutritional facts

Per Serving: 198 Cal (22% from Fat, 5% from Protein, 73% from Carb); 2 g Protein; 5 g Tot Fat; 1 g Sat Fat; 1 g Mono Fat; 40 g Carb; 1 g Fiber; 17 g Sugar; 128 mg Calcium; 2 mg Iron; 158 mg Sodium; 0 mg Cholesterol

Peaches with Part-Skim Ricotta

serves 4

ingredients

1 cup part-skim ricotta cheese
2 cups of peaches
4 tablespoons slivered almonds
1 tablespoon maple syrup
1/4 teaspoon almond extract

cooking instructions

Mix the ricotta with the maple syrup and almond extract.

Equally divide the peaches among four bowls. Top with flavored ricotta and sprinkle the slivered almonds.

nutritional facts

Per Serving: 183 Cal (45% from Fat, 20% from Protein, 34% from Carb); 10 g Protein; 10 g Tot Fat; 3 g Sat Fat; 4 g Mono Fat; 16 g Carb; 2 g Fiber; 11 g Sugar; 199 mg Calcium; 1 mg Iron; 77 mg Sodium; 19 mg Cholesterol

Sardines with Edamame

serves 2

ingredients

1 can sardines (about 4 ¼ ounces)
1/2 cup cooked Edamame
1/4 lemon, juiced
Salt and pepper to taste

cooking instructions

Roughly chop the sardines in a bowl. Mix in the Edamame and lemon juice. Season to taste and serve immediately.

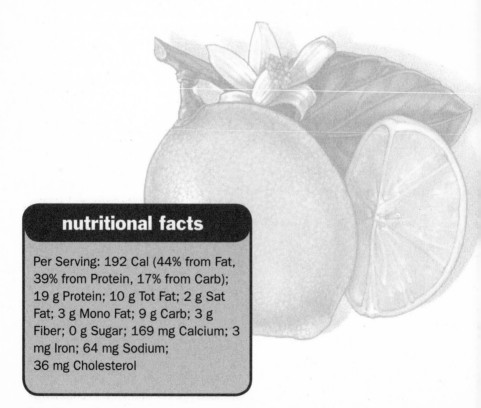

nutritional facts

Per Serving: 192 Cal (44% from Fat, 39% from Protein, 17% from Carb); 19 g Protein; 10 g Tot Fat; 2 g Sat Fat; 3 g Mono Fat; 9 g Carb; 3 g Fiber; 0 g Sugar; 169 mg Calcium; 3 mg Iron; 64 mg Sodium; 36 mg Cholesterol

Ricotta Cheese with Apricots

serves 1

ingredients

1/4 cup low fat ricotta cheese
1 tablespoon apricot preserves
Two drops of almond extract
2 apricots, chopped

cooking instructions

Mix the ricotta cheese with the apricot preserves and almond extract.
Transfer to a serving bowl, top with the chopped apricots, and serve
immediately.

nutritional facts

Per Serving: 166 Cal (23% from Fat,
18% from Protein, 57% from Carb);
8 g Protein; 4 g Tot Fat; 2 g Sat Fat;
2 g Mono Fat; 26 g Carb; 2 g Fiber;
18 g Sugar; 182 mg Calcium;
1 mg Iron; 69 mg Sodium;
15 mg Cholesterol

Yogurt with Flaxseeds

serves 1

✓ *For added flavor, try using fresh fruits/ berries, preserves, compotes, nuts/seeds or vegetables such as cucumber or pureed avocado with a drizzle of olive oil or walnut oil.*

ingredients

1/2 cup low-fat plain yogurt
1 tablespoon ground flaxseeds

cooking instructions

Mix the yogurt with the flaxseeds and serve immediately.

nutritional facts

Per Serving: 116 Cal (27% from Fat, 30% from Protein, 43% from Carb); 9 g Protein; 4 g Tot Fat; 0 g Sat Fat; 1 g Mono Fat; 13 g Carb; 3 g Fiber; 10 g Sugar; 263 mg Calcium; 1 mg Iron; 98 mg Sodium; 2 mg Cholesterol

Sugar Snap Peas with Salmon

serves 4

ingredients

1 tablespoon olive oil
2 cups sugar snap peas
2 garlic cloves, minced
1 lemon
4 ounces salmon, thinly sliced
Salt and pepper to taste

cooking instructions

Remove strings along both lengths of the sugar snap peas. Heat a wok with the olive oil over medium heat. Add the garlic and sauté quickly. Add the sugar snap peas and sauté until almost tender. Add the salmon and sauté quickly. Sprinkle with lemon juice, season to taste, and serve immediately.

nutritional facts

Per Serving: 144 Cal (31% from Fat, 28% from Protein, 41% from Carb); 11 g Protein; 5 g Tot Fat; 1 g Sat Fat; 3 g Mono Fat; 16 g Carb; 5 g Fiber; 4 g Sugar; 118 mg Calcium; 2 mg Iron; 27 mg Sodium; 11 mg Cholesterol

Broccoli with Pumpkin Hummus

serves 8

ingredients

2 tablespoons almond butter
2 teaspoons flaxseed oil
1 tablespoon lemon juice
1 teaspoon ground cumin
1/2 teaspoon ground coriander
2 cups cooked garbanzo beans
2 cups cooked pumpkin purée
1 garlic clove, pureed

1 teaspoon paprika
3 pounds broccoli
Salt to taste

cooking instructions

Combine all the ingredients, except the broccoli florets, in a food processor. Mix until very smooth and thin out with water as needed. Serve with broccoli florets.

nutritional facts

Per Serving: 134 Cal (21% from Fat,
19% from Protein, 60% from Carb);
7 g Protein; 3 g Tot Fat; 0 g Sat Fat;
1 g Mono Fat; 23 g Carb; 7 g Fiber;
4 g Sugar; 113 mg Calcium;
2 mg Iron; 149 mg Sodium;
0 mg Cholesterol

Tofu Cornbread

serves 8

ingredients

16 ounces soft tofu
2 eggs
3 tablespoons canola oil
1/4 cup honey
1 cup instant low-fat milk powder
1/4 cup whole wheat flour
1/2 teaspoon salt
1 ½ teaspoon baking powder

1/2 teaspoon baking soda
1 ½ cup cornmeal
2 jalapenos, finely chopped
2 ounces grated white cheddar cheese
2 tablespoons cilantro, minced

cooking instructions

Preheat the oven to 425°F.

Place the tofu, eggs, oil, honey, milk powder, flour, salt, baking powder, and baking soda in a blender. Mix until smooth. Stir in the cornmeal, jalapenos, cheese, and cilantro. Pour the mixture in an oiled pan. Bake for 25 to 30 minutes. Slice and serve immediately.

nutritional facts

Per Serving: 269 Cal (35% from fat, 15% from Protein, 50% from Carb); 10g Protein; 10g Tot Fat; 3g Sat Fat; 5g Mono Fat; 34g Carb; 2g Fiber; 10g Sugar; 130mg Calcium; 2mg Iron; 419 Sodium; 69mg Cholesterol

Desserts

Often associated with high calories, **desserts should be considered a treat.** One exception to the rule is fruits, which are powerful anti-oxidants and should be eaten every day. For that reason, fruits are the dessert focus of this book. **Give preference to berries, citrus, kiwis, and all yellow/orange/ red/dark colored fruits.** However, be careful of possible allergies, particularly with strawberries, citrus, and kiwis. Whenever possible replace sugar with honey, maple syrup, or agave syrup. **A combination of organic plain low-fat dairy products and fruits** are also healthy dessert choices for providing calcium to your body.

Pomegranate and Strawberry Parfait

serves 2

✓ *Option: Add 1 tablespoon of ground flaxseeds per serving.*

ingredients

1 1/2 cup strawberries
2 ounces pure acai, no sugar
added
1 teaspoon vanilla extract
1 cup low-fat Greek yogurt
2 tablespoons pomegranate seeds

cooking instructions

Mix the strawberries with vanilla extract and acai. Marinade for 30 minutes. Spoon half the fruit mixture into four parfait glasses. Top with yogurt and finish with the berries. Sprinkle with the pomegranate seeds and serve immediately.

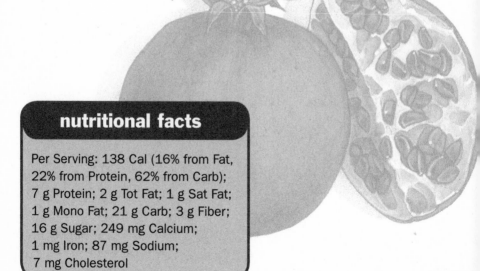

nutritional facts

Per Serving: 138 Cal (16% from Fat,
22% from Protein, 62% from Carb);
7 g Protein; 2 g Tot Fat; 1 g Sat Fat;
1 g Mono Fat; 21 g Carb; 3 g Fiber;
16 g Sugar; 249 mg Calcium;
1 mg Iron; 87 mg Sodium;
7 mg Cholesterol

Cherry Compote with Vanilla Ice Cream

serves 4

ingredients

1 pound English or
Montmorency cherries
3 ounces sugar
1/2 cup water
1/4 teaspoon almond extract

1/4 teaspoon arrowroot or cornstarch mixed with a little water
2 cups low-fat vanilla ice cream

cooking instructions

Remove cherry pits and stalks. Place the cherries in a
pan, add the water, sugar, almond extract, and bring to a
boil over medium heat. Simmer for 10 minutes. Thicken
with the arrowroot mixture and remove from heat. Cool
and refrigerate. Divide among four bowls and top with
the ice cream.

nutritional facts

Per Serving: 263 Cal (8% from Fat,
6% from Protein, 86% from Carb); 4
g Protein; 2 g Tot Fat; 1 g Sat Fat; 1
g Mono Fat; 58 g Carb; 2 g Fiber; 52
g Sugar; 138 mg Calcium; 1 mg Iron;
76 mg Sodium; 4 mg Cholesterol

Yogurt with Prunes

serves 4

ingredients

1 pound prunes
3 ounces sugar
12 ounces water
16 ounces low-fat Greek yogurt

cooking instructions

Soak the prunes in water for two hours. Transfer to a pan, add the sugar, and bring to a simmer over medium heat. Reduce heat and continue to cook for 1 hour. Remove from heat and let cool. Refrigerate until cold.

Divide the yogurt into four serving bowls, top with the prunes, and serve immediately.

nutritional facts

Per Serving: 144 Cal (2% from Fat, 18% from Protein, 80% from Carb); 7 g Protein; 0 g Tot Fat; 0 g Sat Fat; 0 g Mono Fat; 29 g Carb; 0 g Fiber; 28 g Sugar; 247 mg Calcium; 0 mg Iron; 91 mg Sodium; 2 mg Cholesterol

Tapioca Pudding with Apricots and Almonds

serves 6

ingredients

2 3/4 cup low-fat milk
1/3 cup sugar
3 tablespoons minute tapioca
1 egg, beaten
1 ½ cup apricots
2 ounces almonds
1 teaspoon lemon zest

cooking instructions

Place the milk, sugar, tapioca, and zest in a saucepan. Let stand for 5 minutes. Heat and bring to a boil over medium heat, stirring constantly to avoid scorching. Remove from heat and mix in the egg. Add the apricots and almonds. Cover with plastic wrap and refrigerate until use.

nutritional facts

Per Serving: 230 Cal (27% from Fat, 12% from Protein, 61% from Carb); 7 g Protein; 7 g Tot Fat; 2 g Sat Fat; 4 g Mono Fat; 37 g Carb; 2 g Fiber; 29 g Sugar; 168 mg Calcium; 1 mg Iron; 147 mg Sodium; 9 mg Cholesterol

Cottage Cheese with Fruit

serves 4

ingredients

1/2 cup low-fat cottage cheese, chilled
1/4 cup blackberries
1 tablespoon dried apricots
1 tablespoon raisins
1 teaspoon ground flaxseeds

cooking instructions

Mix the cottage cheese with the flaxseeds. Add the blackberries, dry fruits, and serve immediately.

nutritional facts

Per Serving: 169 Cal (19% from Fat, 40% from Protein, 42% from Carb); 17 g Protein; 4 g Tot Fat; 1 g Sat Fat; 1 g Mono Fat; 18 g Carb; 3 g Fiber; 9 g Sugar; 101 mg Calcium; 1 mg Iron; 461 mg Sodium; 9 mg Cholesterol

Papaya Brulée

serves 2

ingredients

2 small papayas
4 teaspoons brown sugar

cooking instructions

Cut the papayas in half and remove the seeds. Spread
the sugar over each half. Place under the broiler and grill
until caramelized. This is pretty quick, so keep an eye on
the papayas. It will take approximately 1 minute.

nutritional facts

Per Serving: 145 Cal (2% from Fat,
4% from Protein, 93% from Carb);
2 g Protein; 0 g Tot Fat; 0 g Sat Fat;
0 g Mono Fat; 37 g Carb; 5 g Fiber;
26 g Sugar; 76 mg Calcium;
0 mg Iron; 12 mg Sodium;
0 mg Cholesterol

Pears with Roquefort Cheese

✓ *If Roquefort is not available, substitute with Gorgonzola.*

serves 4

ingredients

4 pears, sliced
4 ounces Roquefort cheese, crumbled
4 tablespoons chopped walnuts

cooking instructions

Divide the pears among four plates. Sprinkle with the cheese, walnuts, and serve immediately.

nutritional facts

Per Serving: 218 Cal (53% from Fat, 13% from Protein, 33% from Carb); 8 g Protein; 14 g Tot Fat; 6 g Sat Fat; 3 g Mono Fat; 19 g Carb; 4 g Fiber; 11 g Sugar; 205 mg Calcium; 1 mg Iron; 514 mg Sodium; 26 mg Cholesterol

Apple with Almond Butter

serves 1

ingredients

1 apple
1 tablespoon almond butter

cooking instructions

Cut out four pieces of apple around its core.
Spread with the almond butter and serve
immediately.

nutritional facts

Per Serving: 153 Cal (51% from Fat,
6% from Protein, 43% from Carb);
3 g Protein; 9 g Tot Fat; 1 g Sat Fat;
6 g Mono Fat; 18 g Carb; 2 g Fiber;
11 g Sugar; 48 mg Calcium;
1 mg Iron; 2 mg Sodium;
0 mg Cholesterol

Pumpkin Harvest Bread with Ice Cream

serves 16

ingredients

1 ½ cups flour
1/2 cup cornmeal
1 ½ teaspoon baking powder
1 teaspoon baking soda
1/4 teaspoon salt
2 teaspoons ground cinnamon
1/2 teaspoon ground nutmeg
1 cup solid pack cooked pumpkin
(fresh or from organic can)

2 eggs
1 cup packed brown sugar
1/4 cup vegetable oil
1/4 cup apricot preserves
1/2 cup raisins
1/2 cup walnuts
4 cups low-fat vanilla ice cream

cooking instructions

Preheat the oven to 350° F.

Combine the flour, cornmeal, baking powder, baking soda, salt, cinnamon, and nutmeg in a bowl. Beat the pumpkin, eggs, brown sugar, oil and preserves in a large mixing bowl. Incorporate the flour mixture and blend until well mixed. Stir in the raisins, walnuts, and transfer to a greased and floured loaf pan. Bake for 50 to 55 minutes or until wooden pick inserted into the center comes out clean. Cool in pan for 5 to 10 minutes. Transfer the loaf to a wire rack and cool completely before slicing. Serve each slice with 1/4 cup low-fat vanilla ice cream.

nutritional facts

Per Serving: 264 Cal (26% from Fat, 8% from Protein, 66% from Carb); 6 g Protein; 8 g Tot Fat; 2 g Sat Fat; 2 g Mono Fat; 45 g Carb; 2 g Fiber; 30 g Sugar; 127 mg Calcium; 2 mg Iron; 211 mg Sodium; 36 mg Cholesterol

Fruit Juice Popsicles

serves 2

ingredients

3/4 cup pomegranate juice
1/2 cup orange juice
4 ounces acai, no sugar added

cooking instructions

Mix the juices in a blender.
Transfer to popsicle molds
and freeze.

nutritional facts

Per Serving: 120 Cal (25% from Fat,
5% from Protein, 70% from Carb);
2 g Protein; 4 g Tot Fat; 1 g Sat Fat;
0 g Mono Fat; 22 g Carb; 0 g Fiber;
17 g Sugar; 10 mg Calcium;
0 mg Iron; 7 mg Sodium;
0 mg Cholesterol

Dates with Almonds

serves 4

✔ *You may also store each portion in a plastic bag for a healthy prepared snack.*

ingredients

8 dates
4 tablespoons almonds

cooking instructions

Divide the dates and almonds in 4 dessert plates and serve immediately.

nutritional facts

Per Serving: 165 Cal (15% from Fat, 5% from Protein, 80% from Carb); 2 g Protein; 3 g Tot Fat; 0 g Sat Fat; 2 g Mono Fat; 36 g Carb; 4 g Fiber; 32 g Sugar; 45 mg Calcium; 1 mg Iron; 1 mg Sodium; 0 mg Cholesterol

APPENDIX A

Meal Diary and Sample Menu

Meal Diary

Create a journal that you will complete every day to track your eating habits. No worries, you won't have to do this all your life. It might take you a while to figure things out, but eventually you will no longer need to write things down. You may include the following columns:

Date	Time	Food	Drink	Mood/ Pain level	Where you ate	Calories

An eating journal allows you to learn a lot about your own eating habits. It may help you to discover what you are doing wrong and to make appropriate adjustments on your own. You will be in a better position to design your own personal healthy eating habits and meals. You also will be able to provide great information to your medical provider who, in turn, will be in a better position to help you.

Here are a few examples of what you may observe by keeping a journal:
• You ate the wrong foods when you are stressed, at work, or at parties.
• You ate 500 calories over your daily allowances
• You ate a food which is on your allergy list
• Instead of eating a healthy breakfast, you just grab a cup of coffee and go

- You ate out and got sick afterwards
- You are skipping meals

What you find out may surprise you. This awareness of your habits will lead to positive changes. One simple change can make a huge difference in your well-being. Don't be overwhelmed, just look at your journal with objectivity and start to see where you can make a change. Start with one thing. Once you do, and feel great about the result, move on to the next one, and so on.

Sample Menus

The following menus have been designed to show you how you can plan and vary your meals while still staying within your recommended daily calories. Please feel free to adjust them to your preferences. Most of the recipes are based on the right amount of healthy fat, so you don't really have to worry about the amount. Feel free to use smaller portions of soups, salads, or vegetables recipes for snacks. If you need to lose weight, remember to consult your physician or registered dietitian. Discuss what is appropriate for your personal situation. Do not guess on your own, or you can jeopardize your health.

Meal	Recipe	Yield	Calories	Calcium
Breakfast	Granola w/Raisins & Dates (page 42)	1 serving	365	184
Lunch	Salmon & Asparagus Salad (page 69)	1 serving	354	395
Snack	Yogurt 4 ounces berries	1 serving	137 74	488 35
Dinner	Chicken Curry (page 97)	1 serving	480	101
Dessert	Pomegranate & Strawberry Parfait (page 130)	1 serving	138	249
Total calories and calcium			1548	1452

Meal	Recipe	Yield	Calories	Calcium
Breakfast	Cream of Millet (page 43)	1 serving	384	525
Lunch	Broccoli Soup (page 55)	1 serving	178	212
	Tomato, Mozzarella, and Basil Salad (page 68)	1/2 serving	158	230
Snack	Cottage Cheese w/Fruit (page 134)	1 serving	169	101
Dinner	Tofu w/Stir-fried Vegetables (page 92)	1 serving	263	177
Dessert	Pears w/Roquefort Cheese (page 136)	1 serving	218	205
Total calories and calcium			1370	1450

Meal	Recipe	Yield	Calories	Calcium
Breakfast	Muesli w/Peach & Almonds (page 44)	1 serving	211	467
Lunch	Chicken Salad w/Fruit (page 71)	1 serving	385	105
	Yogurt		137	488
Snack	Oysters Stew (page 57)	1 serving	167	201
Dinner	Pork Chops w/ Sauerkraut (page 102)	1 serving	462	142
Dessert	Tapioca Pudding w/ Apricots & Almonds (page 133)	1 serving	230	168
Total calories and calcium			1592	1571

APPENDIX B

Substitutions

Sometimes it may be hard to find certain ingredients. What if you just ran out of one ingredient while preparing a dish, you are allergic to one ingredient and need a substitution, or you want to reduce the calories of a recipe? The following substitution list will be very useful during those times. Use simple judgment to choose the right substitution, depending on the application. Keep in mind every ingredient has a specific function in a recipe and making substitutions may alter the recipe. Baking is particularly a concern since it is all about chemistry. You may have to try a recipe many times before finding the right balance. Bes sure to take notes so you can remember what you did, especially when it turns out great!

Substitution List

1 tsp. allspice	½ tsp. cinnamon, ½ tsp. ground cloves, and ¼ tsp. nutmeg
1 tsp. baking powder	¼ tsp. baking soda plus ½ tsp. cream of tartar
1 cup butter	a little less than a cup of oil
1 cup buttermilk	1 cup plain yogurt Or 1 cup milk plus 1 Tbsp. lemon juice or vinegar Or 1 cup milk plus 1¾ tsp. cream of tartar
1 cup ketchup	1 cup tomato sauce, ½ cup sugar, and 2 Tbsp. vinegar

1 cup chili sauce	1 cup tomato sauce, ¼ cup brown sugar, 2 Tbsp. vinegar, ¼ tsp. cinnamon, dash of ground cloves, and dash of allspice.
1 oz. unsweetened chocolate	3 Tbsp. Carob powder plus 2 Tbsp. Water
1 cup cream cheese	1 cup part skim milk ricotta cheese or low-fat cottage cheese mixed until smooth or 1 cup of creamy or soft tofu plus a little lemon juice.
1 cup half-and-half cream	1 cup evaporated milk
1 cup cream	1 cup evaporated milk
1 cup heavy cream	2/3 cup buttermilk plus 1/3 cup oil or ½ cup part-skim milk ricotta cheese plus ½ cup nonfat yogurt
1 cup heavy cream will give 2 cups once whipped.	In some recipes, substitute 1 cup of creamy or soft tofu plus a little lemon juice. Replace 1 cup of whipped cream with 1 cup of evaporated nonfat milk placed in the freezer until icy and then whipped with a little vanilla powder. This is not very stable; use, as an example, to accompany fruit salad.
½ tsp. cream of tartar	1½ tsp. lemon juice or vinegar
1 large egg	2 egg whites
1 Tbsp. flour (for thickening purposes in cooking only)	1½ tsp. cornstarch or potato starch Or 1 Tbsp. sweet rice flour Or 1½ Tbsp. rice flour Or 1½ Tbsp. granular tapioca Or 2 tsp. quick-cooking tapioca Or 1½ tsp. Agar Or 3 tsp. bean flour Or 1½ tsp. Guar Gum Or 1 tsp. Xanthan Gum
1 cup all purpose flour (for cooking and not baking)	Or 1 cup tapioca flour Or ½ cup soy flour plus ½ cup potato starch flour Or ¾ cup cornstarch Or ¾ cup garbanzo flour Or ½ cup nut flour Or 7/8 cup rice flour Or 7/8 sorghum flour (Milo) Or 1¼ cup rye flour Or 1½ cup oat flour Or 1 cup corn flour Or ¾ cup coarse cornmeal ¾ cup potato starch flour

When baking, these substitutions do not necessary work well by themselves. Usually other ingredients from the recipe need adjustment. Unless you have a lot of time on your hands for trial and error, do not attempt to create baking recipes but rather use those already available in cookbooks in specialty stores or over the Internet.

1 Garlic clove	1/8 tsp. garlic powder
1 Tbsp. fresh grated ginger	1/8 tsp. powdered ginger
1 Tbsp. fresh herb	1 tsp. dry herb
1 tsp. lemon juice	½ tsp. vinegar
1 cup mayonnaise	½ cup yogurt plus ½ cup mayonnaise (canola preferably) Or 1 cup salad dressing such as vinaigrette Or 1 cup low-fat sour cream Or 1 cup low-fat yogurt Or 1 cup low-fat cottage cheese pureed in a blender until smooth
1 cup milk	½ cup evaporated milk plus ½ cup water Or 1 cup buttermilk plus ½ tsp. baking soda (for baking decrease baking powder by 2 tsp.) Or 4 Tbsp. whole dry milk plus 1 cup water Or 1cup other liquid
1-cup molasses	1 cup honey
1 Tbsp. prepared mustard	1 tsp. dry mustard plus 2 tsp. vinegar
Oats	Old-fashioned rolled oats and quick oats are interchangeable.
1 cup uncooked rice or pasta	3 cups cooked
A couple shreds of saffron	dash of turmeric mostly for color, but not quite the same flavor
1 cup sour cream	1/3 cup buttermilk plus 1 Tbsp. lemon juice plus 1 cup cottage cheese blended Or 1 cup low-fat yogurt Or 1 cup cottage cheese plus 2 tsp. lemon juice blended

1 cup granulated sugar	1 cup light brown sugar Or ½ cup molasses (reduce liquid in recipe by ¼ cup) Or ¾ cup honey (reduce liquid in recipe by ¼ cup and add ¼ tsp. baking soda) Reduce oven by 25° F when baking Or ¾ cup maple syrup (reduce liquid in recipe by ¼ cup and add ¼ tsp. baking soda), Or ¾ cup fruit juice concentrate (reduce liquid in recipe by 1/3 cup and add ¼ tsp. baking soda) Reduce oven by 25° F when baking. Or substitute only ½ of the sugar with ½ cup fruit puree Or 1 cup granulated fructose Or 1 cup liquid fructose. Reduce liquid in recipe by ¼ cup.
1 cup tomato juice	½ cup tomato sauce plus ½ cup water or vegetable stock
1 15 oz. can of tomato sauce	1 6 oz can of tomato paste plus 1 cup water
1 cup tomato soup	1 cup tomato sauce plus ¼ cup water or vegetable stock
1 tsp. vanilla extract	1 vanilla bean split and simmered in liquid from recipe
1 cup wine	1 cup stock
1 Tbsp. active dry yeast	1 cake compressed yeast or 1 package active dry yeast
1 cup plain yogurt	1 cup buttermilk Or 1 cup cottage cheese blended until smooth Or 1 cup low-fat sour cream Or 1 cup low-fat goat yogurt Or 1 cup low-fat soy yogurt

APPENDIX C

References and Resources

References

Dunne, Lavon J., *Nutrition Almanac*, Fifth Edition. McGraw Hill Companies, 2001.

Evans, Lee K. and Chris Rankin, *Giant Book of Tofu Cooking*. Sterling Publishing Co., Inc., 2000.

Lorig, Kate and David Sobel, *Living a Healthy Life with Chronic Conditions*. Bull Publishing Company, 2006.

Pappa, Apostolos and Marie-Annick Courtier, *The Saint-Tropez Diet*. Hatherleigh Press, 2007.

Resources

American Diabetes Association
ATTN: National Call Center
1701 North Beauregard Street
Alexandria, VA 22311
800-DIABETES (1-800-342-2383)
www.diabetes.org

American Dietetic Association
120 South Riverside Plaza, Suite 2000
Chicago, IL 60606
800-877-1600
www.eatright.org

American Heart Association
7272 Greenville Avenue
Dallas, TX 75231
800-AHA-USA-1 (800-242-8721)
www.americanheart.org

National Osteoporosis Foundation
1232 22nd Street N.W.
Washington, D.C. 20037
800-223-2226
www.nof.org

National Osteoporosis Society
www.nos.org.uk

International Osteoporosis Foundation
www.iofbonehealth.org